A fearless caterpillar grazed the leaves of the passion flower. His sharp mandibles nibbled tiny holes in each tender leaf. Early morning dew sparkled in the sunlight accentuating his yellow and black stripes as he wriggled his long, slender body across each skinny blade. There was a certain determination about the mission of the caterpillar. At times he stopped to rest before continuing his search for the sustenance of transformation. Mesmerized by this striking and unsuspecting creature, I watched him slither rhythmically across the leaves. My vigil was cut short as other things beckoned me on. Several days later, I searched in vain for the caterpillar. Days passed before I would return again in hopes of seeing him weave his sleek body from leaf to leaf. This time, I found a small grayish colored sack suspended from a shoot on the passion flower vine. It was a translucent cocoon that sheltered the body of some unknown gestating creature. I hoped to witness the hatching of this new life but that was not to be on this day. I left the cocoon to sway in the gentle breeze.

The next morning, as the sun warmed the earth, I returned to find a magnificent butterfly resting on a bed of green near an exotic purple passion flower. The fanning of his fragile orange and black wings was episodic as he prepared for his brave solo flight.

We wait in anticipation for life emerging from the cocoon. Is it -

A Hungry Caterpillar?

A Beautiful Butterfly?

Or Something in Between?

Running
Without A Soul

By Donna N. Miles

In Honor of:

My beautiful daughter, Michelle Brecht
My inspiring and loving granddaughter, Mickenzie Bush,
Her gentle husband, Gary Bush, and
My dearest friend, soulmate, and husband, Larry L. Miles

And:

All who read my story.

"Namaste"

This work expresses opinions unique to the author's experiences in the last seventy-five years. In no way, does she claim these writings to be the reality of others. They are her gift to the generations who are to inherit the wisdom of the world as she knew and lived it. In the words of philosopher, educator, Samantha Norman, "It is when you have the courage to draw strength and wisdom from the reflections of your past that you can bask in the joy of today and prepare for the challenges of tomorrow."

Illustrated by Mickenzie M. Bush

Published by:

FriesenPress
Suite 300 – 852 Fort Street
Victoria, BC, Canada V8W 1H8

www.friesenpress.com

Distributed to the trade by The Ingram Book Company

Table of Contents

Part One / The State of The Nation   xi

Part Two / Growing A Moral Society   79

Part Three / Author's Note   119

Acknowledgements   123

I heard an interesting story about an American hunter in search of big game in Africa. It seems the hunter and his spirited guides were running indefatigable in search of big game. Without warning, the hard running native guides stopped running and sat down on the nearest rock. The American protested. He pleaded and begged and tried to bribe the runners. The native guides would not get up and continue the search. In frustration, the American hunter questioned why the guides refused to get up and hurry on in search of the big game. He was told the men had run so fast they had left their souls behind. They needed to wait for their souls to catch up. Could it be that one of the problems our society faces today is that it has out run its soul?

A nation that has out run its soul is at risk of losing the morals and ethics embedded in the fiber of who it is and who it can become. These are the beacons of hope that strengthen the decency of a civilized society without which we risk running past the most significant parts, events, and relationships in our lives. Our children are the most vulnerable casualties of the race. Many times we rob them of their God given right to a warm, gentle, safe childhood. In the blindness of our quest, we sacrifice the quality of their lives to continue the search for 'bigger game."

Part One

The State
of
The Nation

1.

I believe in preserving the sacredness of all life and I believe that the birthing transformation for us as human beings is much like that of the most ordinary of creatures. It saddens me to see the deterioration of honor, respect, and moral values that once were pervasive in our society. This is evidenced by the small measure of regard we afford children and childhood. I've heard it said that children are our future. If that is so, and I believe it is, it is critical that we nurture in them the moral values of goodness, truth, faith, compassion, and civility that once made our nation great.

Life is meant to evolve in a predictable, orderly, and timely fashion. Exceptions to this premise happen when alien forces attempt to sabotage the process. When the natural rhythm of life is interrupted to force into being a helpless creature, we deny the sacredness of life. The same is true when hostile entities sabotage the processes of life to coerce into being ideological disciplines. Honor and respect are disavowed for human beings when, most of the time, decisions are made to support a desire for expediency. In general, expedient decisions are used as tools of manipulation and intimidation to impose one person's will upon another. This happens many times in the political arena. How many times have you heard, on television, the tongue of the wily politician coercing his subjects to support his actions? Often attempts toward breaking the rhythm of the process to insure a desired outcome leaves a bad taste in the mouths of constituents and diminishes faith in those leaders. At what price and at what point does manipulation become corruption? When did mankind claim the right to alter the outcome of a birthing process? At what point do we stand idly by as evil consumes the inherent goodness of man? My conscience tells me our nation is at risk of losing its soul.

'Life is what happens when you're busy making plans' is a tidbit of wisdom I found somewhere. A lot has happened in my seventy-plus years of life. Some planned. Most not planned. Much of what you will read on these pages is intended to expose the dramatic events that have colored my life as well as the life of our culture and our nation. I hope to present evidence that reveals my understanding of how our nation and the world has evolved in my lifetime. My intentions in these writings are personal and somewhat selfish. They are anecdotes that offer distinct characterizations of the generations of my lifetime. I hasten to say that it is not my intent to presume or even suggest that everyone in the varying generations fit or embrace the profiles offered here.

I believe each of us is obligated to shed a glimmer of light on the past. It is our gift to the generations who are to inherit the wisdom of the world as we knew and lived it. Samantha Norman, philosopher and educator, once said, "It is when you have the courage to glean strength and wisdom from the reflections of your past that you can bask in the joy of today and prepare for the challenges of tomorrow."

In the evolution of our nation these seventy-plus years, I have witnessed the dramatic deterioration of the values and ethics of the United States. By that I mean, the respect we offer one another, the language we use to communicate, the decency and honesty we practice in our dealings with each other, and the simple courtesies we extend to others. Much of the erosion may be attributed to flawed leadership. Some may be accredited to the fluidity of the culture. In the coarse of the years, the nation has been blessed with strengths that surpass all other societies. Sometimes efforts to move the nation forward have been wrought with disastrous decisions that have stained who we are as a democracy. Before we agree to 'throw in the towel' and surrender to a subordinate culture, I would like to suggest that we re-invent our educational system. I am convinced that educating our young with the desired ethics, morals, and sacred regard for human life is the key to grow a responsible, compassionate society. Change in a culture must have its roots in the soul of man. Much of what I share scrutinizes the political and the secular by using the chronology of Presidents as a tool to outline the significant events and milestones familiar to my time and place in the world. I chose the Presidents as a guide through my history and the history of the US. Presidents are the leaders of governments and as such their behaviors, policies, and morals make a difference in who a nation becomes. They provide a virtuous model of all that America symbolizes in the world. They can choose to either enhance or damage the image of this great nation. You will learn more about this as you read about those who have been Presidents of the United States in the last seventy plus years.

2.

The Constitution of the United States gives power to the president to be the commander-in-chief of the nation. His is a legalistic role. He is to exercise that power in making sure all the laws are fair and equitable for the citizens, to insure laws constituted by the people are carried out, to report to the nation the state of the union, and most importantly, to inspire the people and the nation to greatness. It is his job to preserve and protect the freedoms, liberties, and well-being of all in the nation. In my lifetime, some have guarded the rights of these powers with their very souls. Others have been careless in their vigilance and have brought shame upon the nation. Then there are some who have mis-used these powers for their own political agenda.

The way I see it, the purpose of government is two-fold. First, it is to nurture optimism and hope in man's eternal search for new visions of the future. Second, it is to assist in the creation of an *institution* of structures and laws that support the societal needs of the *community* it serves.

Sometime ago I read where someone compared the *institution* of religion and the *community* of parishioners as two necessary entities in organized religion. The presumption was made that, *institutions*, by nature, operate out of head ideology, vulnerable to becoming evil and can crush the heart and soul of *community* because *community* is born out of the heart. In these writings, I will use these two distinctive terms to compare the *institution* of government and the *community* it serves. Do we not have evidence of how *institution*, the government, can crush *community*, the population?

I hasten to say that I believe the United States was born out of the hearts and souls of men who lived by a profound sense of goodness, honor, and integrity. It was their intent that priority be given to the preservation of respect, dignity, and freedom of all people.

As I see it, the structure of the United States government is that of three branches; the Executive, the Legislative, and the Judicial. The Judicial branch is involved with the legalities of the nation. The Legislative branch is made up of the House of Representatives and the Senate. The Constitution vests the power of the Executive Branch of the nation with the President. I think that should mean the

President is to act as the arbiter of balance between the *institution* and the *community*. For that to happen, the President needs to be a person whose heart rests with the welfare of the entire nation - a person who operates with wisdom and care to insure that neither the *institution* nor the *community* overpowers the other - a Statesman who pledges a neutral position in managing the affairs of the state - a person whose allegiance is to nurture and maintain the greatness of America - a person who inspires the nation to greatness - a person who ponders before strategizing. (Pondering is going within the depths of one's soul to discern what is right. Strategizing is examining issues to determine appropriate responses.) Unfortunately, all this is contingent upon the nature of a human being committed to defending and honoring the Constitution of our democracy. The President is usually aligned with one party or the other and therefore makes many decisions that reflect the wishes and desires of that party. That is where corruption and evil present themselves.

More than two hundred years of struggle between the *institution* of government, the *community* of mortals, and the flawed judgment of leadership has chipped away at the confidence, faith, and determination of this strong nation. America is a nation different from all others. It is a nation with a soul and a heart. We must never forget that. Several years ago, a minister titled his sermon, "Let no one seize your crown." I think the meaning of his sermon pertains to individuals and *institutions* alike. For our nation, I believe a way to interpret that statement is to say, "Let no one seize from America that which makes it a unique beacon of hope in the world." I would carry that statement further and say, "Let no one seize your crown, especially not a charismatic personality or a cult personality. To do so puts your soul at risk and rational thought is diminished." We must never sacrifice the inherent goodness in the soul of our nation.

3.

In 1913, I was not a dream in anyone's heart. Life in America was simple and easy. People were proud of the role America played on the stage of civilization. It was the year Woodrow Wilson was elected the twenty-eighth President of the United States. He embraced the policy of neutrality toward conflicts in other nations. It was the policy supported in the early 1800's by Thomas Jefferson, the third President of the United States. Thomas Jefferson urged neutrality, but not isolationism. He pursued a policy of "peace, commerce, and honest friendship." That laudable policy was honored until 1914. Germany and her allies, Austria, Hungary, Italy, and Russia, were engaged in a struggle with Great Britain and Germany's policy of unrestricted submarine warfare threatened to block America's commercial shipping. When Germany sank the British passenger ship, the Lusitania, killing a number of American citizens, President Wilson dropped the position of neutrality which allowed the United States to reluctantly enter World War I. Three of my uncles were drafted into the military and served in that skirmish. Thankfully, they returned with few scars to remind them of what they had experienced. One served in the medical corps. After his return, he enrolled in medical school at Baylor University in Waco, Texas where he became a respected dentist and an adjunct professor in the School of Dentistry. Another resumed his life on the farm and one returned to live out his dream of becoming a brakeman on the Union Pacific railroad.

Even though the war happened before I was born and my parents were not personal victims of its atrocities, my life was colored by their accounts of its horrors. World War I ended in 1918 with the signing of a truce that marked the declaration of peace, but discontent in Europe continued to lurk on the horizon.

Life in the U.S. was euphorically smooth until the crash of the stock market on Wall Street on Tuesday, October 29, 1929. Black Tuesday marked the beginning of the Great Depression. The devastation of this economic disaster shattered the optimism and financial gains of the bull market. Hope for financial security was denied. People languished in the wake of their losses. It was reported the despair of this crisis led some investors to leap to their deaths from multi-storied buildings.

At first glance, it appeared my family would not have been inconvenienced by the sudden drop of the market. How far can the value of nothing drop? My father was a barber. Even though he worked long hard hours, twenty-five cents a haircut and ten cents a shave provided a scant livelihood. Mother was a teacher whose salary ranged between twenty-five and fifty dollars a month. They operated on a limited day-by-day subsistence. Prices for marketable farm goods, wheat and livestock, dropped to dramatic lows during the depression. Farmers were faced with little or no way of providing the necessities for their families. Of course, that meant farmers couldn't afford the twenty-five cents for my father to cut their hair and school districts couldn't pay teachers. It was a bleak time.

On the heels of the depression and concurrent with the grief of economic ruin, was a crisis equal to, if not more disastrous to, the heartland of America. Severe weather conditions ravaged the midwestern states of Oklahoma, Kansas, Texas, and parts of Colorado and Nebraska. Clouds refused to produce rain, unbelievably hot temperatures parched the earth and abusive winds created an inferno threatening all living organisms. Hundreds of acres of soil took flight in the strong winds causing walls of dust to cross the land. Sagebrush broke free from the clutches of the earth to form huge lattice barriers. Fences were lost under inordinate banks of dirt much like snow in a blizzard. The plains were enveloped in massive clouds of red, silt-like dust for weeks, months, and years. Lack of rain meant crops dried up denying a food supply for humans and livestock. Ponds, streams, and wells ceased to run. Families went without water. On Black Sunday, April 15, 1935, a gigantic dust storm ripped and twisted across the earth with power not unlike a tornado or hurricane. Mountainous clouds of dust engulfed the area making the simple act of breathing difficult. People died of pneumonia and starvation. It was a dark time in the history of our nation.

To emphasize the length of time the residue of the Dust Bowl remained, in 1963, my husband, Larry, our daughter, Michelle, and I lived in Liberal, Kansas. One Sunday afternoon, when returning from a few days in Oklahoma, we drove in strong, dust-laden winds. Dust blackened the blue sky. Particles of sand pummeled the car. Waves of dust washed over the highway. Fence lines stood like mounds of chocolate snow. Larry turned on the lights of the car and maneuvered through the blinding storm. Upon our arrival home, we discovered the wind had sucked open the windows of the house and had covered everything with a heavy layer of fine, gritty silt. The color of the sofa was hidden under the dust. Many times when we lived in Liberal and parked our cars on the street, sand sifted through the window casings and concealed the color of the upholstery. Recurrences of dust bowl events gripped the vast western plains for multiple years.

In a small town in northwest Oklahoma, my family struggled against the remnants of nature's violence. My daddy owned and operated the only barbershop in the area. Under the desperate circumstances and charging a mere penance for a haircut, he barely put food on the table for my mother and my two siblings. And, many times, just when you think things are stretched beyond toleration, along comes an unexpected blessing. It was on August 24th, 1936, the hottest day of the year according to my mother, that twins joined the family. One child was expected; two arrived. In those days, without sophisticated medical technology, many things were shrouded in the mystery of happenstance. Those were the conditions under which I entered the world. In a town less than small, the birth of fraternal twins brought a new kind of excitement. An aura of specialness surrounded multiple births. Whenever we went out, people would stop to visit, then turn and look at my brother and me. With a breath of awe, they would say something like, "And these are the twins?" At the same time, and as my parents attempted to adjust to our seemingly rare birth, news of trouble in countries across the ocean trickled into the United States.

Every day around the dinner table Daddy would tell us about the happenings in the world; between haircuts and shaves he would read the newspaper in his barbershop. Since we had no radio reporting the current news, Daddy was our eyes to the world. He told us about the despair and unrest escalating around the globe. Germany and Japan were behaving like horses 'faunching at the bit' as they began flexing their muscles in anticipation of taking control of smaller, defenseless countries. In 1939, Germany imposed itself upon Czechoslovakia and Poland. Soon other surrounding nations were under the control of their demonic governing. Each conquest served to empower Hitler as he put in place ideologies that would restrict the freedoms of the people. Hitler was beginning a surge that would force his bold claim of a single party dictatorship based on totalitarian and autocratic ideals of national socialism on all of Europe.

A radio would not have done us any good as we had no electricity. Rural Electric Association (REA) lines didn't extend to our farm until December 4, 1944. I can still see the line man mounting a meter on a tall post and hanging the lines that would surge electrical power across our farm. Since we had relied on an Aladdin kerosene lamp to light our dark nights, we were thrilled when they flipped the switch that brought us a step closer to what most folks took for granted. We basked in the yellow glow of the single light bulb hanging in the center of the room. On that day, I grabbed a pencil and wrote the memorable date on the wallpaper adorning our kitchen. Mother never said anything, but I suspect she was less than thrilled. To cover my impulsiveness would have been costly, so we lived with the reminder for several years. Since it had been so long in coming to our farm, electricity was never taken for granted. Light in the darkness of night was a luxury. To conserve energy, Mother and Daddy insisted we turn lights off when we were not in the room.

Financial resources were in a perpetual state of flux and almost a fantasy for my family. We lived off the productivity of the land, my father's barbershop, and my mother's teaching salary. When I was young, my mother was promised forty dollars a month to teach in a one room country school. Many times, instead of a paycheck, she was given a discounted warrant that was redeemable for a portion of the contracted amount with a promise the remainder would be paid sometime later, but often that didn't happen. This made life difficult for our family. Rothenberger's grocery store allowed us to carry credit by the month. We were poor, but I never remember going to bed hungry. I had faith in my parent's ability to provide for us. It was a time when people lived with a sense of frugality. In the summertime, Mother canned vegetables from the garden and stored them in the storm cellar Daddy dug in the side of a hill near the kitchen door. Every so often a crew of neighbors would assist my father in butchering a calf or a pig to provide meat for the family. I remember those as difficult days. My father was tall in stature; tender in heart. He grieved over the sacrifice of an innocent animal. In the spring, Mada Rumsey, the rural postmistress, would deliver a box containing one hundred day-old baby chicks to our front door. The back seat of her car was stacked with boxes of these tiny, down-covered, chirping fuzz-balls to be delivered to neighbors along her route. To insure their survival, we kept them in a makeshift pen behind the wood stove in our dining room. Later in the spring, after they had grown enough, we moved them to a small brooder house. It was my job to attend to their needs - food of chicken mash, fresh water, and a routine cleaning of the brooder. I spent hours watching the activities of these creatures of nature. In mid June, when the chicks had grown to a tender size and it was time to process them for table food, I was sad. Each of us was expected to help mother with this project. I hope I don't have to do that again, but thanks to the tutelage of my mother, I know I could if circumstances required it of me. We did what we had to do to survive. I am grateful for the lessons of measured living, preserving, conserving, and making things from scratch with elements at our disposal. It concerns me that, today, most young people rely on prepared foods from the grocery shelf. I wonder about their ability to survive in times of disparity. Still, I have faith in the genius of their creative minds. They would be all right.

When I was young, written communications and numerical computations were done on red Big Chief tablets instead of computers. In place of I-Phones, telephones hung on the wall. They were connected to switchboards answered by the warm and courteous voice of an operator saying "Central." If you were fortunate enough to have a telephone, you shared a line with several other people and were assigned a ring code-specific to your home. My grandparents had a telephone. Their ring was - two longs and a short. One long ring summoned the telephone operator (Central) who in turn connected you with the person with whom you wished to speak. Almost at any given time, you could lift the receiver from the hook and listen in on conversations between your neighbors. Even though most people in our rural *community* had telephones, we didn't have one until about 1954. Despite the fact that we had no Wal Mart or Best Buy and no I-Pod or computer, life was good. Today, technology and supposed affluence entices us to be a 'throw-away' society. If we don't like something, we throw it away and get something else. I use the term supposed affluence because so much of what we possess is not of need, but of desire and is made possible with a plastic card. Do I want to go back to the days of my childhood? No! But, my heart aches for children to know the simple, carefree, slow-paced days of my youth. Today, life in a child's world, evolves around the multiplicity of activities that consume their every waking moment and leaves little time for probing the mysteries of life.

After World War I, America resumed its policy of neutrality toward taking sides in international conflicts. Neutrality is good in theory, but when human lives are endangered, when human dignity is sacrificed, well-intentioned policies that attempt to legalize responsibility become irrelevant. Compassion becomes the moral guide and we must take sides. Neutrality helps the oppressors, not the oppressed. To live in peace and to act out of goodness was all the citizens of the United States expected of their government. We perceived the role of the U.S. was to stay out of the business of other nations and become involved only when human life was threatened with uprisings fueled by evil. Reports of ethnic cleansing pricked the moral fiber of the U.S. and led to rethinking our neutral position. We have never been a nation with the stomach to stand idly by and witness acts of cruelty inflicted on innocent human beings. The thunderous rumblings of discontent for the pain and suffering of others pounded at the door of our conscience.

President Franklin Delano Roosevelt (FDR), the thirty-second President of the United States, was inaugurated and served between 1933 and 1945. He was the only President to serve four terms before term limits were ratified in 1951. On December 7, 1941, a heinous act of aggression was committed against the U.S.. The Imperial Japanese Navy attacked our ships docked in Pearl Harbor, Hawaii. Several ships were sunk, almost 2,500 persons were killed and many others were wounded. Japan hoped this despicable act would discourage the U.S. from entering the war they were planning to wage in Southeast Asia. It resulted in making the exact opposite happen.

The United States was outraged by this senseless tragedy. We were a nation of unrealized strength and resolve. On December 8, 1941, President Roosevelt, took off the gloves of neutrality and isolationism and declared war on Japan.

Three days later, December 11, 1941, Germany declared war on America. Roosevelt authorized the military to do what it could to rescue those being persecuted in Europe, hence the U.S. found itself in World War II. This is sometimes referred to the 'War of all Wars' because many nations around the globe were either directly involved or suffered the effects of the atrocities. It was a grueling war. The heart and soul of America was on the line and everyone at home and abroad 'put their shoulder to the grindstone' to support our troops' efforts to restore the freedom of the oppressed. World War II chipped away at the confidence held for our leaders when Roosevelt dropped the policy of neutrality. Fueled by faith in God and a somewhat diminished faith in decisions of the government, the resolve of the people to rescue those who were being brutally murdered was bolstered.

The government took advantage of the Military Draft System created in 1926 to organize man-power for the nation's military force. At age eighteen, young men were required to register with the Draft Board and most were eager to serve. They lined up to volunteer for service. They believed it was their duty to stand for the freedom of our nation. They served with honor. Men were ranked according to their ability to serve. A 4A ranking meant a young man was fit to serve. Those with a 4F ranking were not subject to the draft. Many times young men of this ranking were declared physically unfit to go to war. My father was deemed exempt from military duty because he had four young children. Women picked up the slack for men fighting on the front lines. They went to work in factories making airplane parts. They served as nurses and joined the Red Cross, an organized crisis relief agency. Their sacrifice awakened the cause for women to enter the work force outside the home - a circumstance that continues today. After the soldiers returned home, some women were reluctant to forfeit their role in the work force. Women grew accustomed to the luxury of a second salary to supplement the family's income. Women's Liberation has declared every woman's right to pursue a career outside the home. Today's women have greater opportunities to seek higher education degrees that qualify them for professions as corporate executives, doctors, lawyers, and entrepreneurs of any number of small business endeavors. As time has gone by and with the worsening of the economic climate in the U.S. and with the family's desire for a higher standard of living, one salary is not sufficient.

It is right to ask, what about the children? During the war years with dad away and mom working, children were usually placed in the loving care of extended family members. Today many young children spend the day or at least a portion of the day in daycare outside the home. Do you ever wonder what role this has played in shaping the lives of our young and of our society? Since I was never a product of a daycare experience, it is hard for me to imagine what that must be like. My mother worked as a teacher. Either she or my dad was handily present to care for me. Today that is not always an option. For years, I have pondered this dilemma. More about that later.

My brother-in-law, Jack, served in the army. He was stationed in the Marshall Islands most of the time. Jack was gone from the family for three long years. There were no cell phones or computers to keep in touch then. Letters from home were savored like the sweetness of a Snickers candybar. While he was away, Nola, his sweetheart, now wife of sixty years, kept busy doing what she could to help in the war effort. Fort Riley, the military base near Junction City, Kansas, stood as an ever present reminder of the consequences of war. It was there that young men were transitioned from training to service. Nola participated in the United Service Organizations (USO). The mission of the USO was to provide morale, welfare, and recreation-type services to uniformed military personnel. Nola sent letters of encouragement and gift boxes of homemade cookies and candies. On Friday evenings, she went to the Armory and danced with the service men. Nola was a soft-spoken, squeaky-clean moral, fun-loving young woman. Down through the years we have often teased her about her contributions to the morale of the soldiers while Jack was away. Everyone did what they could to lift the spirits of those who served.

As children, we brought our pennies to school to support the Red Cross which helped care for our young soldiers. Women gathered to rip old sheets into strips, rolled them together and sent them to the Red Cross to be used as bandages in caring for the wounded. Many people invested in war bonds to help defray the cost of the war effort. Some revenue from pie suppers went to help our military. In case, you don't know, box suppers and pie suppers were fund raising events in local schools. Women and girls prepared a box lunch or a special pie to be auctioned to the highest bidder. Children in the school entertained with skits of music and drama. Other revenue raised from these events was used to support various causes such as: educational supplies for the local school, financial support of the Red Cross or to help sustain a family whose life circumstance was in crisis. The proceeds from pie suppers were allocated to specific societal needs. During the War, that meant a charity related to supporting the troops.

Families eager to do their part endured the rationing of food items. One week day was when we could get bacon - something special for us. Mother would send one of us children, either by foot or bicycle, down the hot, sandy road to pick up our two pounds of bacon. On other days, it was the same scene when we claimed our share of butter and sugar. Rubber was scarce because the military needed all the rubber it could get to maintain equipment used in the war. The nation pulled together like no other time in my life. A sense of loyalty bound neighbor to neighbor. In many ways, it was a romantic time in the history of our nation; it was a euphoric time when love and camaraderie was the glue that held all of us together. We had an honorable cause; we had a reason to sacrifice that others might live in freedom. We were proud to be Americans because to be an American meant to be strong and brave in times of turmoil. It meant to live with conviction in preserving the honor and dignity of all who were oppressed. We were a United nation. Life was tough, but each of us felt a sense of pride in the strength of our unity as a nation. Our voices were gentle and sincere. Kindness was in the air. We were bound together with love, compassion, honor, and respect. America was humbled in its greatness.

I remember many times we would come upon a soldier with his duffel bag draped over his shoulder, standing by the roadside, hitching a ride home. My father, and most others, would stop and inquire, "Where are you going, son? Hop in. We can take you as far as Chester," or to wherever we were going. Since our family of six filled to capacity the space in our 1934 Ford, Daddy might offer, "Throw your bag in the back and hop onto the running board." Then he would drive with extra caution to provide a safe journey. Occasionally he would throw negligible responsibilities to the wind and take the soldier to his desired destination. Riding short distances on the running board of a car was common-place then. Safety regulations make this illegal today. I must hasten to tell you that, in the forties, cars like ours were not designed for the comparable speeds of today. Sometimes, a young man might even spend the night before continuing on. And, if the soldier wanted a haircut, he was sure to get a free one from Daddy. That was a time when people did what they needed to do to work together and to survive. It was a time when people shared from the generosity of their hearts. It was a time when our service men were honored - almost revered. Today, it makes me sad that our young fight for our freedom and we fail to grant them the gratitude and respect they have earned. I am sorry circumstances make it unsafe for us to extend hospitality to everyone.

When I drive down Pennsylvania Avenue in Oklahoma City, I go by the Village Library. Standing erect and addressing the U.S. flag that flies overhead is the bronze statue of a young man. On the platform where he stands is a message that proclaims, "UNITED WE STAND." That pretty much tells it all. In my early years, America was committed to protecting freedom and justice for all.

Every morning, in the one-room school, we stood erect before the stars and stripes, with hands over our hearts, to repeat the Pledge of Allegiance to the United States of America. Be sure, it was a pledge that came with the expectation of loyalty to defend our nation against those who would threaten our freedom. On a deeper, more profound level, it was more than that. The unspoken pledge was one whose seeds were at home in the heart and soul of each of us calling us to commit to be the best person we could be, to live with goodness and honor. I am sorry that both of these are becoming a part of our history instead of a reality for today and I mourn the deteriorating passion toward the allegiance to the United States. Patriotism calls us to an honest search for the truth. It does not require us to hate those from other countries, nor does it suggest that we should live with our eyes closed to the indiscretions of our own. It calls us to humility and respect. We have failed to provide our children with common educational exposures of who we are as a nation and to inspire their dreams of who we can become. In many cases, we have neglected to transmit the vision of the free, democratic, society our country has struggled to become.

It is necessary that we remember the ravages of evil lest we fall prey to complacency and sanction evil as good. Entering World War II changed the nation from simple and easy to an America marked by perseverance and sacrifice.

It was right for us to take pride in the role our nation played in making the world a safer place.

4.

Adolph Hitler was an Austrian-born German politician and leader of the National Socialist German Workers Party commonly known as the Nazi Party. In some respects, he was a foreigner to the country. As a youth he exhibited no extraordinary personal magnetism. Hitler was seen as an oddity - a figure of scorn and ridicule. In today's world, he may have been labeled a 'nerd.' By 1919, even though he became the object of boundless, mass adulation, he was hated by his political enemies. His rise to power was due less to his 'charismatic personality' and more to a Germany traumatized by the impotency of a lost war, the revolutionary upheaval, political instability, economic misery, and cultural crisis. Hitler might have been perceived as a nobody, but in those peculiar circumstances, his thirst for power merged with the despair of a scorned society. Germany longed for a leader to change its image from a nation defeated in World War I to a nation accentuated by its radical power. His charismatic personality became 'charismatic authority.' He was Germany's hope to regain its prominence on the world stage. Who else to do that than a charismatic personality with a cold-hearted, blood-thirsty desire for power? Thus it was, in 1930, Hitler was appointed Chancellor of Germany and became a 'charismatic domination.'

Hitler ruled Germany as an absolute dictator. He espoused German nationalism, anti-semitism, anti-capitalism, and anti-communism. His most effective tools were charismatic oratory and propaganda. Hitler's strongest desire was to establish a "New Order." He forced upon the nation a single party dictatorship based on totalitarian and autocratic ideals of national socialism. Within three years, Germany and the Axis powers occupied most of Europe. Nazi forces engaged in numerous violent acts and systematic murder of as many as several million civilians. An estimated six million Jews were targeted in the Holocaust and between five hundred thousand to one million of various other nationalities including Romanians, Poles, Soviet civilians, Soviet prisoners of war, people with disabilities, homosexuals, Jehovah's Witnesses, political and religious opponents and anyone else who questioned Hitler's power.

I believe this is what happens when good men yield to evil and allow someone, or some ideology, to steal their crown of goodness. Germany was a nation that lost its moral compass. Morals are born out of the soul. When they are lost the soul suffers from the disconnect of its original goodness.

Does any of this sound familiar? Think about it.

Sixty-five years after Hitler's rule, Germany continues to struggle with the humiliation, disappointment, and shame over the Holocaust that denied six million Jews their lives. As painful as those memories are, it is imperative we remember lest we be seduced into repeating the heinous violations of man's inhumanity to man.

In the 1940's, movies cost ten cents for children under the age of ten. Popcorn was also a dime. My siblings and I were privileged to go to the movies often. After settling into our chosen seats, a newsreel previewed the news of the last few days or weeks. Much of the news focused on the events of World War II. Images of soldiers trudging through the cold and wet in mud-laden boots - military weapons over their shoulders, trains carrying gaunt, hollow-eyed people too emaciated to fear their destination, smoke rising from the infernos of death, and long, deep trenches filled with the bodies of victims of hatred, were displayed on the screen. The accounts of those ghastly scenes were seared into the fiber of who I was to become. I sometimes wonder why my parents allowed me to be exposed to the raw evidence of man's venomous behavior. Perhaps they wanted me to know that sometimes evil happens in the world. Today, we hope to protect our young from the burdens of shameless horror. This is a good thing.

Anyone who had first-hand or vicarious experience with any part of this horrendous time in our history knows the realities of the savageries of the Holocaust. Still, today, there are those who deny the despicable acts that mark the Holocaust. Theirs is an organized propaganda movement strategized to rewrite history and minimize its facts. They massage and manipulate truth to sabotage the convictions and beliefs held by the global *community*. They would call themselves "revisionists." Others might refer to their movement as "negationism," defined as a denial of historical crimes against humanity. It is an attempt to negate truth. For whatever reasons, their ultimate goal is to shake the confidence of those who hold well-known beliefs in hopes of persuading them to embrace 'evil as good.'

In the 1940's, the U.S. took a deep pause before entering the disputes of other nations. As the years have passed, the world has become less user-friendly, and governments more strident and impatient, the pauses are shallow, more like weary sighs. The world's expectations of our nation are like those of a child nagging for a piece of candy in the grocery store.

5.

I was five years old in 1941. At that time, life in rural northwest Oklahoma came with the blessings of honesty and integrity. On Saturday mornings, during cotton-picking season, Mr. Craighead would drive his pick-up truck into town. He would invite any child who wanted to earn a little money picking his cotton to get on board. He promised to pay ten cents per pound. He offered no written contract, only his word. With a peanut butter sandwich and perhaps an apple packed in a syrup bucket and a long cotton sack pulled across our shoulders, we would clamber onto the bed of his truck. At the end of the day, Mr. Craighead would weigh up the cotton each of us had picked. If our pick was ten pounds he placed a one-dollar bill in our hot, sweaty hands. He settled up with each child according to the amount picked. Now, at times, Mr. Craighead was a crusty character who held our feet to the fire, but we were willing to work for him because we knew he was fair and we could trust his word. He honored young children. I regret that this is not always the case in today's world.

My father never knew how my little ears received the details of the stories of heinous war crimes committed on unsuspecting people. I feared being separated from my family. When airplanes flew over the house, I was anxious. Daddy always planted a two-acre plot of land with the seeds of watermelons. It was the summer of 1944. If you know anything about gardening, you know you can't afford the luxury of weeds cohabiting with tender young plants. On periodic occasions each of us would grab a hoe and take to the watermelon patch. One day, a couple of hours before dusk as World War II raged in Europe, my family set about to get the weeds out of the rows of melons. I was seven, almost eight, years old. Managing the long handle of a hoe was a bit of a challenge. Mother and Daddy had mastered the art of using a hoe. My older brother, sister, and my twin had progressed in their skills of hoeing and could cover more ground than I. I was slow and had a hard time keeping up. At one point, when I looked up into the approaching darkness I could barely see the darkening shadows of Mother and Daddy in the distance. I was overwhelmed by the fear of being lost from the safety of their protection. Fear drives a nail in the heart of innocence and infects the world. This was one of my fearful experiences of evil in the world. Only those who are evil; understand evil.

Those horrific visions are stored in the compass that guides my search for what is right and what is real in the world. To say my life was negatively affected is an understatement. The devious, despicable images of evil crimes inflicted on innocent people remain with me. I can't imagine the thoughts and fears of those who lived in the midst of that devastating, dark time in the history of the world. Since I was a little girl, I have been on an eternal quest to learn the truth, whatever the truth might be. I am prone to dig in the recesses of issues and events for evidence that points to reality. Those times when I have mis-calculated or have been blindsided by a difficult circumstance have been painful for me. It is my belief that my faith in who I am as a spiritual being is eroded when I skim the surface of reality. Skimming the surface, puts me at risk of losing myself in the great abyss of nothingness. That is frightening. My faith in Someone greater than me empowers my confidence to trudge forward in search of what is right, of what is real, and of what is true. I believe this to be the blessing that has come from the horror of my childhood images of war and for this, I am grateful.

6.

Most of what I knew about President Franklin Delano Roosevelt was filtered through my parents. In late 1944, President Roosevelt won an unprecedented fourth term as President of the United States. On January 20, 1945, he and his Vice Presidential running mate, Harry S. Truman, took the oath of office in the presence of a small gathering of people. Roosevelt was in poor health. He lived with the infirmities of polio. I remember President Roosevelt's wife, Eleanor. She was a tall, slender, graceful figure - an advocate of social issues that affected the quality of life of ordinary people. I think it is fair to say she believed in Social Justice, a view that everyone deserves equal consideration. Even though her husband was known to have extra marital affairs with several young women, Eleanor conducted herself with grace and dignity while carrying out the duties of the First Lady of a great nation. When the President was stricken with poliomyelitis, she tended to him devotedly. She made a career of being his political helpmate. She had a strong, persuasive personality. My parents were so enamored with President Roosevelt and his wife, Eleanor, they named their first daughter after her.

On April 13, 1945, a few short months after taking office for his fourth term, Roosevelt died and Vice President, Harry S. Truman, was sworn in as the thirty-third President of the United States. He was a gentleman from Missouri who brought an honest, straight-forward, determined presence to the Presidency.

President Truman was the first President I remember with any clarity. He was short in stature and wore a perky chapeau on top his head. He walked with a quick step and spoke with the same cadence. His approach to decisions was direct and was executed with precision. A sign on his desk in the oval office read, "The Buck Stops Here." He believed that whoever was President was responsible for making the final decisions in matters before the nation. He was supposed to have said, "No one can decide for him. It is his job."

When President Truman came into office, he had not been briefed by President Roosevelt on the development of the atomic bomb or the unfolding difficulties with Soviet Russia. Those and a host of other wartime problems became Truman's to solve. He told reporters, "I felt like the moon, the stars, and all the planets had fallen on me."

Presidents Franklin D. Roosevelt and Harry S. Truman were charged with the unbelievable task of dealing with the atrocities of World War II happening in several countries. The two most significant were Germany and Japan. President Truman made some of the most crucial decisions in history. World War II started when Germany attacked Poland on September 1, 1939. The dreadful horrors of War with Germany ended on V-E Day (Victory in Europe) May 8, 1945. It wasn't until August 15, 1945, that Japan surrendered to the U.S. This date is known as V-J Day (Victory in Japan.)

The war with Japan had reached its final stage soon after Truman took office. An urgent plea to Japan to surrender was rejected. On August 6, 1945, after consulting with his advisors, Truman ordered atomic bombs dropped on Hiroshima and later, Nagasaki, two cities that supported World War II. After the loss of thousands of our young men, the surrender of Japan, the rescue of innocent persons being held hostage in horrible concentration camps in Germany, and with the self-inflicted death of Adolph Hitler - the most evil man of his time, these two wars came to a final conclusion.

I believe historians got it right in their assessment of the effects one evil personality can have on a vulnerable society. Germany was destitute. Hitler came to power proclaiming his vision to restore Germany's image as a strong, productive nation. Unfortunately, without morals and ethics, evil spirits can't restore goodness that is not imbedded in them. Hitler's cruelty of forced assimilation and genocide inflicted irreparable damage upon the soul of Germany.

Had President Truman not taken the drastic steps that would end World War II many more lives would have been lost. My parents admired Truman's courage to act. As I remember it, President Truman's time in office was marked by his quiet, decisive acts and his attention to social needs - expansion of Social Security, a full-employment program, a permanent Fair Employment Practices Act, public housing, slum clearances, and civil rights. Harry's time in office embraced and instituted entitlement programs that supported Social Justice.

My parents believed in Harry Truman's ability to lead the nation. That is easy to understand. They belonged to the Democrat Political Party and embraced the strengthening of social programs. The priority nestled deep within their souls was that government be mindful of the needs of the people. I don't think they would take pride in being Democrats today. It is a different Party today than it was then. In the forties, it was the Party of the *community* of people. And, the Republican Party appeared more like the heavy-handed *institution*. I believe the Democratic Party has been hijacked by deceptive, power hungry, roguish personalities. It has become the heavy-handed *institution* while the Republican Party appears to be the Party of the people. In my view, the Republican Party supports limited government, respects and honors the rights and needs of the people, works toward a balanced budget, is dedicated to the practice of prudent spending, and provides for equal employment opportunities. With these claims, it characterizes the *community*. Harry might find this a very disappointing turn of events. I liked Harry. He seemed real and ordinary. Most people of my era remember scenes of Harry playing the piano. He entertained guests in the White House with his light-hearted musical presentations. Oh, how we need a Harry today - one who is determined to protect the *community* of America and one who takes delight in the amazing gifts of the people!

President Truman's presence, demeanor, and honor was good for the United States.

His wife and First Lady, Elizabeth 'Bess' Wallace was a more retiring figure who stayed in the background. She maintained the home fires holding their tight-knit family together while Harry conducted the business of the nation.

7.

Before World War I, I suggest the U.S. was seen as an infant nation struggling for a clear sense of identity. It was a nation that had not claimed its place in the global world. The Civil War had been about clarifying how people of the states could live together and was a time of beginning to fine-tune a governmental structure that would honor the rights and privileges of all our citizens. Even though President Abraham Lincoln, the sixteenth president of the United States between 1861 and 1865, signed an act on April 16, 1862 that abolished slavery in Washington, D.C., it has remained 'the elephant in the room' holding each of us hostage to the prejudices of our ancestors. In my lifetime, multitudes of courageous people have made meaningful contributions toward eradicating this horrible blight. Rosa Parks and Martin Luther King are among those who have dared to stand in the face of inequality to claim freedom for all. The "elephant" of racism is smaller now than in 1936 when I was born. Still, there are those of all colors who continue to scratch at the wound of racism to keep it oozing with infection. It has become a political chip bandied about recklessly to manipulate the populace. Remembering the lurid historical acts perpetrated upon the most vulnerable of our society comes with a sense of guilt and sadness. Some suggest reparations to exonerate those who suffered at the hands of slavery. Would taking from the heirs of perpetrators to give to the heirs of the perpetrated take away the anger and resentment stored in memory banks? Will money erase generations of memories from the past? When did we come up with the idea that money can cure all our problems? At what point do we allow the past to consume the present? Are we willing to sacrifice our present to live in the past? I believe the majority of people in today's world are color blind. I have faith in the ability of the heart to live in harmony with one another. I suggest we let love heal the brokenness of our nation. The "elephant" will eventually be ushered out the door and taking its place will be a dove of peace that holds the promise of freedom and justice for all.

Our granddaughter lives in Alabama. About a month ago, we visited there. As we drove through the countryside, I had a profound sense that we were treading on sacred ground. The scenes from movies of the South came to life with visions of innocent, brave, black families in horse-drawn wagons making their way along dusty roads under a canopy of the massive magnolia. A mental image appeared of those gathered under a tent of weeping cypress singing soulful, yet jubilant, songs of revival and praising their God who promised to be with them always. A gentle breeze released the sweet fragrance of the magnolia in bloom. All this was reminiscent of the aura of courage that once prevailed in this place and the beautiful spirit of hope that protected the oppressed. When I returned from my imaginings, I was grateful that the pain surrounding the shameful days of slavery was beginning to fade into the pages of history.

The honorable success of World War II declared the United States the only remaining super-power with courage, resolve, and resources to make a positive difference in the midst of strife. The expectations accompanying that title placed us in the role of Savior of the World. Sometimes that has brought us joy and other times it has been a burden too heavy to carry. We are strong. We are compassionate. We are willing to risk the dangers of war that others might live in peace. I am proud to live in a country whose heritage is woven together with threads of care and concern for others. At times, when our heartstrings have been plucked and other nations have relied on us to solve their problems, we have responded more like over-indulgent parents who send money before ascertaining the scope of the circumstances. Then we have been prone to error. But ours is a nation with a heart.

On October 24, 1945, the United Nations came into existence. The purpose was to bring all nations together to work for peace and, based on the principles of justice, to honor human dignity and insure the well-being of all people. It was structured as a vehicle through which member nations could present their cases surrounding the disagreements affecting their countries. The body of nations was expected to wrestle with the scope and validity of the situation and determine a collective resolution. It seems the success we achieved in Europe awakened our nation and the world to the power of a democratic society. I paraphrase a scripture that proclaims, "To whom much is given; much is expected." When the vote is taken regarding how and who can settle disputes, all eyes turn to America. Many times, we send money to attend to the immediate well being of those who are suffering the lack of basic human necessities. Through arbitration we seek to gain agreement and compliance in the world *community*. Sometimes that does not work out and other possible resolutions must be brought to the bargaining table. The nature of the U.S. has always been to aspire to greatness in whatever endeavors it choses. It hungers to be the light that shines around the globe and inspires a lasting peace for all. Peace merits a dedication of time and energy to insure its reality. We must never abandon our quest for peace for all mankind. Senator Robert F. Kennedy, brother of the late President John F. Kennedy, the thirty-fifth president of the United States between 1961 to 1963, once made a statement that speaks to his rugged spirit and to that of the American people. He said, "Some people see things as they are and say why. I dream things that never were and say why not?" At the heart of the American people is a spirit that dares to look beyond the 'what ifs' in search of the 'why nots.' Why not peace?

Since World War II, I have lived through times of war on many fronts: Korea, Vietnam, and Bosnia to name a few. Today it seems more palatable to reference war under different names. The first Iraq war was called Operation Desert Storm. Now Operation Enduring Freedom is the war in Afghanistan. When the conflicts surrounding the Bay of Pigs in Cuba, the intervention in Grenada, and the invasion of Panama are included in this list, it averages a war every ten years of my life. That is a bleak picture. For the most part, America's decisions to break from a position of neutrality have been to eradicate the suffering of the powerless. Sad to say, there have been times when the U.S. has been accused of intervening in the struggles of other nations for selfish reasons. There have been too many wars in seventy years! President Dwight D. Eisenhower, the thirty-fourth President between 1953 and 1961, tried to find ways other than war to settle differences that made life unbearable for us. But when force is necessary we must never lose. America cannot be expected to solve the problems of the world nor should it assume to dominate by sheer power. Eisenhower was a commanding general of the victorious forces in Europe during World War II. He brought to the Presidency his military expertise. He was married to Mamie Geneva Doud who was a quaint and interesting First Lady. I can still see images of her precise, coiffed hair, topped by a simple, flat, unpretentious hat. Her presence seemed to fit what I thought of as the typical military wife; the very proper wife. Mamie waited in the wings at home while her husband commanded armies to save lives. She had a warm and easy smile.

A sense of wonder surrounds the expectations of a 'super-power.' Hope is woven into the fabric of wonder. Without hope in someone or something more powerful than we are, we are at risk of falling into helpless despair. As children, our parents assumed that protective role. Many turned to faith in a Supreme Being. Others relied on luck that surrounds us as spiritual beings having a human experience. In other words, they trusted that someone would come to their defense. But who in the family of mankind can come to the aid of a nation of people oppressed by the actions of a maniacal leader? Those to whom much is given, much is expected. The strongest among us is expected to protect the weakest. If the U.S. is the strongest, then it must stand up and claim its role in the global order. It is the sworn duty of the President of the United States and of every citizen to invest themselves in the preservation of the strength of our nation. Without us, hope in a future without fear is lost. Ours is a formidable task, but America has never shirked it's responsibilities. With confidence, determination, and courage, we have stared down the vicious tigers of evil and injustice. President Ronald Reagan, the fortieth president of the United States between 1981 and 1989, once said, "If we lose freedom here, there is no place to escape to."

Just as parents walk a fine line when it comes to intervening in their child's relationships, so does a powerful nation. It is wise to question the circumstances. When does what we intend as 'help' become interference? When does money intended to restore a balance create dependency and a sense of entitlement? These are questions parents grapple with as they help launch their young adults into the world. Our nation must learn the wisdom of pondering these questions before it acts.

8.

Pop! Pop! Pop! In the distance, the explosion of firecrackers followed by the intermittent whoosh of Roman Candles bursting in the air could be heard. The 4th of July celebration was always an exciting time, especially for youngsters. It was a day to frolic and picnic in the park. Perhaps the scene and the conversation in our house on those mornings went something like this. "Hurry up. They're shooting off the fireworks," Marion, my older brother would have shouted, as we'd race out the door. My older sister, Eleanor, would have helped Mother fry the chicken, bake the beans, and slice the watermelon. Earlier in the morning, I would have sat on top of the ice cream freezer to stabilize it while Donald, my twin brother, turned the crank. Homemade ice cream was as much a tradition on this day as apple pie.

It was July 4th, 1946, the first year after World War II officially ended. Everyone in our town and the surrounding area would gather in the park to mark the historic moment of the birth of our great nation. This year, the day promised to be even more euphoric as we were celebrating in the after-glow of a job well done in the War effort. We were proud of our brave young men, many of whom died in the fight to liberate people from the tyranny of persecution at the hands of dictators and despots. There was pride in the united strength of our fellow Americans. We had offered the world a first-hand look at what it means to honor the basic human rights of others.

On this day, there would have been a parade with horses and bicycles and red wagons. Some years, there was square dancing on the greens in the park. Sack races and turtle races on the street in front of Branstetter's Grocery store were among the scheduled events of the day. My bothers would have captured an unsuspecting turtle meandering along the road, marked his crusty shell with fingernail polish for identification and prepared to pit his racing angst against the other turtle contestants. About four o'clock in the afternoon, the town's mens baseball team would challenge a team from a neighboring town. As the shadows of the day began to hang over the *community*, a lone firecracker exploded and children danced in the glow of sizzling sparklers.

July 4th of any year is a time to remember what has made the United States of America a great nation. It is a time to ponder the moral fiber that compels young men and women to answer the cries of the oppressed. Many have given their lives in battles that weren't ours to fight. They did so because they cared.

9.

The events of two World Wars punctured the bubble of security surrounding America. A sense of vulnerability introduced doubt in who we were as a nation. Prior to World War II, the United States was steeped in morals and ethics that were good. Much of what happened was well-intentioned and predictable. Following the war, the escalation of technology and science commanded the reins steering the nation toward creations and inventions beyond most of our imaginations. The nation was relieved the war had ended and proud of its role in protecting the lives of the defenseless. I think it fair to suggest that in some regard we were a little 'puffed-up' in our success. We had a right to be. We had earned it. But maybe it was in that bloated sense of who we were as a 'super-power' that we began seeing ourselves in a grandiose way. It may have been an inflated sense of self that prodded ill decisions and chipped away at the morals and ethics of our founding fathers. I don't know about you, but when I get over confident I behave outside myself and sometimes my actions don't represent the best in me. Then, my good intentions are at risk of being sacrificed for something not so good. Today, our visions of reality are clouded by the creation of gray areas and are shaped by disingenuous deceptions to be perceived as politically correct. This is the foundation that supports the painting of evil as good.

Dwight David Eisenhower was born in a small frame house in Abilene, Kansas. Today the Eisenhower Library, a memorial to him, stands in Abilene near his birthplace. Eisenhower was a five-star General in the U.S. army. He stood with great Statesmen like Winston Churchill, General George S. Patton, and General Charles de Gaulle. Eisenhower was a tall, confident, and commanding presence when he stood before the podium to address the people. From already knowing my fears in World War II, you might know I viewed him with great admiration. He had a steady, comfortable demeanor. Perhaps there were those who didn't like 'Ike,' but I thought the nation was in the hands of a powerful leader. His military prowess spoke volumes to me. It gave me a sense of security. Even my parents, who were staunch Democrats, appreciated what he brought to the nation. When we listened to his strong, assertive voice on the radio, we believed in the possibility of peace for our nation and for others around the globe. In my inexperienced youth, I believed if anyone could do it, Eisenhower could. He was the embodiment of hope that we could solve dreaded issues without war. His honesty and integrity were characteristic of a true Statesman.

10.

My life in the fifties was dominated by high school and college activities. I graduated from high school in May of 1954 and entered a college class-room on June 3rd of that year. By increasing my class loads in summer, winter, and spring semesters, I graduated in three years with a Bachelor of Science Degree in Education. As the baby of the family, I was the last to go to college. My parents had exhausted their financial resources making it imperative I complete my degree quickly and work toward becoming self-sustaining. The diploma certified me to be a teacher of young children. In the fall of 1957, I accepted a teaching position in Liberal, Kansas - one of the best decisions I ever made. Liberal had an excellent school system that supported teachers in their efforts to make a difference in the lives of those under their tutelage.

The Vietnam War broke out in 1955 - media yielded to the pressure of the minority and credited their voices as the majority. Anti-war activists visited Vietnam for the specific purpose of putting the military, thus the government, under a micro-scope to examine the conduct of those who carried out the missions of war. War is not pretty nor are the heinous acts of cruelty and death imposed upon innocent people by despicable dictators. Through slanted and distorted reporting, the media tried the U.S. military in the press and on the television and convicted the nation of all kinds of supposed war crimes. The bottom line of their accusations was that of the imposition of America in a rift between North and South Vietnam. Once again, the nation was asked to re-visit the policy of neutrality. This action by the media ignited a fire of lust for glory in reporting through deception, tainted truths, and the violation of the rights of the innocent. Since that time, the media has claimed the right to manipulate facts and events in favor of the most advantageous voices. The intent of the media was accomplished. It cast a villainous cloud of shame over the U.S. and cast a gray shadow over the honorable intentions of the young men and women who gave their lives to offer freedom to others. It was responsible for discrediting and dishonoring America. That was the first time I remember the media intentionally painting a negative picture of the United States for all the world to see. The media had the blood of America on its hands. Our troops were pulled away from the nation of Vietnam without completing the mission. When the soldiers returned home they were given less than a hero's welcome. Shame on the voices of the media. They got away with disgracing the nation and interfering with the mission to liberate the oppressed. To this day, they have continued to take even more aggressive liberties that create division in the nation. They placed an aura of self-serving guilt around America for the sake of elevating their significance in shaping the nation. Vietnam was the second time in my life when I witnessed our nation wince under the accusations of guilt. Faith lost in the ability of a democratic society to demonstrate honor, trust, and equal justice infects the hearts of its people and puts the nation at risk. Accusations, true or untrue, alter self-perceptions and diminish the power of the adversary. Politicians use this strategy to sabotage the effectiveness of their opponent. They use it to deceive their constituents. Malicious deceit is the root of corruption.

In 1958, nonviolent sit-ins by young black students spread across the nation. Their intent was to lift an awareness of societal inequities that supported the discrimination of the civil and human rights of those forced to live in the margins. The recurrence of this brewing dilemma summoned recognition and change. Even though the intent was one of nonviolence, when patience was exhausted skirmishes broke out. People were injured. People were killed. People lost hope in an impotent government to bring forth meaningful resolutions. The nation's wounds of guilt and shame continued to fester.

Keep in mind, I was a country girl, a naive young woman. Wars and pestilence disturbed my innocence and singed my conscience.

11.

The election of the Massachuetts Senator, John F. Kennedy in 1961, made many in the nation nervous because the Kennedys were a Roman Catholic family. People wondered if, as President, JFK would follow the dictates of the Pope. Today, that is too ridiculous to imagine and given all that has happened since his inauguration, those concerns seem trite.

Kennedy was the second youngest president to be elected in the nation. He was forty-three years old, handsome, and debonair. His wife, Jacqueline, lived with elegant reserve. She was quiet and soft-spoken. They made a handsome couple. Both brought reverent grace and dignity to the White House. History records these years as the 'Camelot Years' when the nation got a taste of what it might be like to have royalty in the Capitol.

The magic of Camelot was not to last forever. It was broken on November 22, 1963, when President Kennedy was assassinated as he rode in an open convertible down Elm Street in downtown Dallas, Texas. Within a couple of hours, Lee Harvey Oswald was arrested and charged with murdering the President. A few days later, Oswald was shot and killed by Jack Ruby. It was an audacious act of horror perpetrated on the nation. With the help of the media, we became first-hand witnesses to those dastardly deeds. For days, months, and years the U.S. was shrouded in grief. The nation was in a state of shock. First, it was abhorrent and surreal that anyone would be so inane as to take the life of the President of the United States. In the study of American history, we learned of the assassination of President Abraham Lincoln. That happened in 1865. Kennedy's assassination was in 1963. The nation was naive enough to believe that all persons living in the U.S. were more honorable and civilized than in the1800's and that no one would be so evil as to harm the President. This was a tragedy that wounded the heart of an unsuspecting nation. Secondly, under Kennedy's watch, there was faith in the political prowess of the government. People believed he was honest and would embrace that which was good for all the nation. Because of his heartfelt connection with the people, his death broke the magic spell of hope for a kinder and gentler nation. His tragic death stunned the nation much like the death of Diana, the Princess of Wales.

Every so often an extraordinary moment in time interrupts the ordinary. President John F. Kennedy was the extraordinary of the sixties. His warm, genuine heart stretched beyond any one political ideology to address the cares, concerns, and needs of all parties. He was the President of all the nation. In some ways, under his leadership, the people lived in a euphoric state. His catastrophic death shattered the dream awakening the soul of America.

Lyndon Baines Johnson, Vice President, the big, tall Texan who wielded 'back-room power' was sworn in as the thirty-sixth President of the United States, immediately after the Kennedy assassination. He and his wife, Claudia Alta Taylor (otherwise known as "Lady Bird"), spoke with the soft drawl of gracious Southerners. Most of his dealings were congruent with the wishes of congress and the people. The nation mourned for days and months. In the immediate days that followed the assassination, First Lady Jackie Kennedy's thoughtful composure was the strength that helped the mourning nation begin the healing process. She had been the wife of the President, but he had been the President of the people. She used that as her compass in making her way through the awful days of grief. Every element of the funeral was rich in symbolism and pageantry, even their four-year-old son's salute to his father's, the Commander and Chief, casket. I can still hear the gentle clip-clop of the riderless horse as he maintained a distinct cadence walking alongside the caisson carrying the President's body down Pennsylvania Avenue. Jackie was mindful of how history would record the event and wanted it to be one that honored her husband, one that honored the nation he loved, and one the nation would never forget.

During the first two years of Kennedy's presidency, Jacqueline assumed the project of redecorating the White House. She believed the White House belonged to the people and it was her duty to preserve its sanctity for all to enjoy. She gathered pieces of art significant to the history of America from the archives and galleries and had them placed in strategic places. When her project was complete, she invited the media to do a walk-through as she did the commentary explaining the significance surrounding each room, the color of the walls, the art work, the rugs on the floor, everything, including the fabric on the furniture. She reminded America of the special events that had taken place in the various rooms. Jackie was among the most gracious First Ladies I have known.

On a cold day in January of 1961, John F. Kennedy's inaugural address was about the greatness of America, the concerns facing the nation, and his dream for a brighter future. He posed a challenge to every citizen, "Ask not what your country can do for you. Ask what you can do for your country." Another way of putting that is to say, don't wait for the country to do everything for you. Do something to make a difference in the country. Today, in Arlington National Cemetery, an eternal flame marks his grave.

12.

I think this is a good time to look at the nature of a few of the generations that have influenced the evolution of the culture and society of America in my lifetime. It is interesting that at the time of Hitler's reign in Europe, the United States tried to maintain a policy of non-interference. To save the lives of those who were oppressed, the nation was compelled to violate its convictions and enter World War II. It was compelled to step outside its life of innate innocence and simplicity and into an unnatural life of power and force. When people are forced to abandon the deep-seated yearnings of their souls, the imprint of the scars of disappointment will, in some way, alter the remainder of their lives. This is what happened to the Greatest Generation of my time.

I believe a look at the generations of my lifetime offers clues to how our nation has become who and what it is today. Members of the Greatest Generation, born 1920 - 1942, helped rebuild the U.S. and the world after the ravages of World War II. During this tough time in our nation, families learned frugality, self-discipline, and the importance of a strong work ethic. Organized religion was accepted as a meaningful part of their lives. They learned the value of faith in a power greater than themselves. They believed that through the ethic of honest hard work they could create their own opportunities. The stark lessons of the wars, they knew, meant a loss of innocence and the necessity of facing one's own mortality. This generation is marked by courage, respect, and inter-connectedness of family and friends. The Great Depression of the 1930's left many families without work and the basic necessities of shelter, food, clothing. From the unprecedented prosperity that followed World War II, people learned the value of a good education and applied a strong work ethic toward the building of careers, the building of homes, and the raising of responsible families. The era of the Greatest Generation is steeped with hardworking, dedicated, honest, moral and ethical people who struggled through two world wars and the depression. A heightened sense of prosperity followed the wars. Many parents were afforded the luxury of a comfortable and affluent lifestyle. They wanted to give their youth what they had to do without during the wars and the depression. I suspect this was the seed of entitlement. For some the message was, you give, we take. They lost sight of the needs of others and became fixated on satisfying the needs of self. Many became arrogant and looked toward to a grandiose future. Some left their souls behind, abandoned the values and precepts of their parents, grabbed the reins of life and began guiding the nation toward a pre-conceived, orchestrated societal revolution. That revolution continues to be underway as I write. Many in this era abandoned belief in a power greater than themselves. Spiritual faith in the God of their creation suffered a disconnect. Organized religion struggled with new paradigms designed to impact the lives of those who determined it meaningless. Little mention is given to their morals and ethics. Their behavior and attitudes have influenced every succeeding generation. More is written about that in my writings of the *Summer of Love* experience.

A look at the musical lyrics of this generation and some that followed emphasize the deterioration of the morals and ethics once held by the previous generations. Much of the music today is loud, erratic, and violent. Some embrace anti-religious doctrine, but don't deny God. Something is terribly wrong with this picture. Some of the feelings of the generation that followed the Baby Boomers and Generation X seemed to believe that government is charged with caring for every basic need. They expected government to provide free lunches. Their misnomer was that government had its own supply of money, and it does except that it comes from the pockets of the people. This is the generation that believed they were sanctioned to change the world. With such ill thought beliefs and given power to implement them, it is easy to imagine their run to crush the soul of the *community*.

Today many in the generations that follow the X'ers run without their souls and with the expectation that other generations will follow suit. No doubt they have changed the world, but some of the changes have left morals and values in the dust of time.

There is another generation that warrants attention. It is the generation of our granddaughter. These carefree, risker-takers want immediate gratification, are good at multi-tasking, live in the moment, are well informed, but are without wisdom and reflection. Theirs is a generation of heightened sense of spirituality. They seek alternative spiritual experiences and work to grow a toleration of organized religion. Today's youth are more worldly than those of earlier times. But they are not necessarily smarter or better able to handle the challenges of being an adult.

I believe the generations and the events of the sixties were the pivotal point that led to the spiraling downward of the morals and the values held sacred in America.

13.

Puzzlement is the best word to describe the events surrounding the *Summer of Love* in the 1960's. As many as 100,000 idealistic young people flocked to San Francisco in search of different value systems and experiences. They were the Baby Boomers who represented a counter-culture aimed at creating a social crisis that would liberate the nation and the world of conventional morals. It was a time of sexual revolution. Those who went to San Francisco were instructed to bring flowers to symbolize altruistic ideals of universal brotherhood, peace, and love. Who could deny those principles? But they were achieved at the expense and loss of the moral compass that held the nation together. The deviant behavior accompanying this new culture tended to fragment, divide, and dismantle the existing morés of our society.

In the beginning, those who participated in that event and other similar gatherings were known as 'hippies.' When the media laid claim to their story, they were called 'Flower Children' as it was their custom to wear flowers, pass out flowers, carry flowers, and decorate with flowers. Many wore flowers in their hair.

The *Summer of Love* influenced the development of a world-wide subculture. When the flower children returned home at the end of the summer they took with them new styles, ideas, and behaviors. In a sense, that gathering and others like it adopted a political ideology that changed our nation and one that espoused the attitude of 'anything goes.' Meaning, anything you choose to do is okay. Young people could sense the hypocrisy of the morés created in the existing social system. They had come face-to-face with a world of crooked politicians, lecherous preachers, ignorant teachers, greedy lawyers, broken marriages, dishonest business deals, and untold rip-offs, scams, and lies. They abandoned the values and lifestyles of their parents.

Perhaps the entertainment industry was more influenced by the *Summer of Love* than any other area of society. Some in the business of entertaining adopted the values and ethics of that movement.

In my young years, the entertainment industry made a distinct difference in my life. Without electricity, the stories we knew were wrapped in the cover of a book and imagined through our experiences. Motion pictures invited us to visually experience a story. Since we lived in the country, our parents didn't feel comfortable leaving my siblings and me home alone at night. On many Monday nights, mother and daddy would go into town for a social gathering. They would give each of us two dimes - one to purchase a ticket at the theater and one for the popcorn. In the early forties, it was safe to allow children the freedom to go to the theater alone. Mrs. Cates, the proprietor of the theater, walked up and down the aisle chastising kids who were slumped in their seats, ones who propped their feet on the back of the seat in front of them, and ones who disturbed the movie. She ran a tight ship and wouldn't hesitate to expel rowdy viewers. She didn't ask them to leave. She ushered them out the door with the promise their parents would be notified. It was a time when most people assumed the responsibility of protecting the safety and innocence of young children. Hillary Clinton was right when she said, "It takes a village to raise a child."

Most movies produced survived the stringent scrutiny of Hollywood producers. Still, our parents held the trump card that determined whether a movie was or was not appropriate for us.

When I was young, story lines in movies involved light drama and funny scripts. Stories were played out on a screen with actors cloaked in dazzling costumes and surrounded by elaborate sets to depict the scenes. Verbal descriptions were in grandmother language. There were suggestive sexual innuendoes but no explicit portrayals. Now it is just the opposite, sexual scenes are explicit portrayals and leave nothing to the imagination. Long ago many Hollywood producers abandoned stringent scrutinizing policies. The mandate that protected the values and morals of our society, particularly those of our young, have been abandoned for the take at the box office.

In my opinion, little magic surrounds the actors and actresses of today. Movie stars of the earlier era remain memorable. I just finished reading 'Good Stuff,' Jennifer Grant's book about her father, Cary Grant, who played mystifying romantic roles in movies. It is a heart warming story about his life. The book is a good read. I wonder how many of those who act in movies today will be remembered in 20 years. Some of todays actors squander their innate talents on roles inferior to their acting potential and many times screen writers create scripts unworthy of their superb talent. Many in the movie and television industry repudiate the integrity of their artistry by choosing to participate in roles that do not champion their passion.

Some roles and scripts today invoke reprehensible language, horrifying violence, and story lines only an idiot would find entertaining. Do they make a difference in society? Of course they do. They reinforce, propagate, and exacerbate the disrespect and common decency once embraced by previous generations. They play a distinct role in inciting the nation to Run Without A Soul.

14.

As I have reflected on the days of the sixties, I believe they represent a rejection of what most in the Greatest Generation accepted as the moral compass of our nation. In some ways, they opened the door to living in euphoria rather than reality. Many were activists who wrote beautiful ballads that told stories about social conditions and solutions for making the world, sometimes specifically America, a better place. Some of these folk singers I remember are: the group called Peter, Paul, and Mary; Anne Murray, Joan Baez; and one of my favorites was John Denver and his song 'Sunshine On My Shoulder.' Some from this era are legends of their time. Today, I am grateful for their gifts of insight and song. I was not a parent of one who rejected all I had believed in. Some of those who were parents then, found it painful and impossible to relate to their children, so they broke with their own values in hopes of re-connecting with their offspring. They abandoned their roles as parents which set their young adults adrift with no anchor. In essence, they cut the cord that tethered them with their children. Parents pulled away the safety net leaving their young stranded in an abyss without a moral compass to find their way back home. In their state of lostness, their young sought comfort in all kinds of abhorrent behaviors - addictive drug use, sexual promiscuity, and cult involvements. The fabric of our society has been weakened forever by this time in history. They achieved what they set out to do which was to create a societal crisis in hopes of making a difference in the world. Some of the differences were good. Some were disastrous.

Parents left their souls behind, changed the world as we had known it, and propelled a comfortable society toward the darkness of social degradation. I believe it was Rahm Emmanuel, former White House Chief of Staff in the Obama administration, who indicated you never want a serious crisis to go to waste. I wonder if this philosophy could be used for *institution* to do things to the *community* which before may have been thought impossible. This was a time of crisis. Some in that era created a crisis to change the world. It is known as the *Summer of Love*.

Could it be our current President authorizes the same tactic to unsettle the economical structure of our nation? First, create a crisis to disconnect the nation from its basic principles, next create a crisis to terrorize the nation and take away its sense of economical security. I believe this can be categorized as the desecration of a nation. It is the kind of distorted manipulation that happens when evil is declared good. Such behavior may destroy man's faith in the *institution* and in the *community*. It is behavior that may divide and destroy our nation. It unscrupulously urges the nation to run with abandon toward the pursuit of an ideology. In accordance, the soul is left behind.

The nation is under a cultural breakdown. Much of it has to do with our children. We live in a society that robs children of the innocence of childhood making them old before their time.

Rites of passage that previously transitioned childhood to adolescence are no longer acknowledged. The social morés dictating when it is appropriate for little girls to begin wearing facial make-up, or nylon stockings with high-heeled shoes, or for little boys to begin wearing long pants have been abandoned. Children are enticed to prematurely assume the roles of an older age. For many, that means they are denied the time to develop age-appropriate social, relational, and behavioral skills. I believe the escalation in the number of our troubled teens can be attributed, in part, to the robbing of their right to a warm and nurturing childhood. Morals and ethics and regards for others are rooted in childhood.

Not long ago, I was reminded of the days when young men were taught respectful behaviors. My husband, Larry, and I were on vacation. We had flown to California. A transfer from one terminal at the airport to another required of us to ride a tram. It was apparent when the doors opened for us to enter the loaded tram that there were no unoccupied seats available. As the vehicle lurched forward, I grabbed the strap hanging from the ceiling to steady myself. A young man in kakis and a knit shirt, jumped up from his seat. "Please take my seat," he said to me.

"Thank you. I'm okay," I countered. He persisted, "My Momma would slap my face if she knew I didn't give you my seat." I didn't want to sentence him to a slap in the face. I was filled with a warm sense of joy and gratitude for a mother who taught her son to respect others and to a son who was thoughtful enough to honor the teachings of his mother. I will hold that young man in my heart forever. To me, he will always be a symbol of hope for a gentler world. Kindness happens when a person has more regard for the well-being of someone other than self and acts on thoughtful instincts.

There is an innate and eternal yearning within the soul of man to maintain a perpetual connection with his original beginnings. In a complex world wrought with imperfections, it is easy to be lured away from our homing instincts to follow the strong voices of those who espouse contrary ideologies. I think, in part, this is what happened with the Flower Children of the sixties. Young people lost faith and confidence in societal role models. Some considered the hypocrisy surrounding the keepers of morals and ethics of humanity. Parents and politicians espoused beliefs in equality, simplicity, and concern for their fellowman but continued to turn a deaf ear to creating solutions to social issues. Those youthful believers hoped that the creation of an audacious crisis would put a spotlight on the ills of society and shock the nation back to its center. Others participated in as many immoral acts as they could think of in hopes of peeling away the layers of sanctimony. Instead, it was like they stretched the tether that connected them to society too far and suddenly found themselves hanging over an irretrievable cliff never to return again. Today, they live with new realities marked with shades of gray. Theirs is a legacy that changed the nation. It is a cancer that infected the morals and ethics of society. The *Summer of Love* lit a fire of dramatic chaos designed to burn away the established mores and social structures. Again, I am obliged to remind you that it was a time when ungrateful youth mercilessly ripped out the hearts of their parents. They ridiculed and scoffed in the face of those who gave them life and all the luxuries afforded by their hard labors. They set out to forge an altered path, a fast track, if you will, that would set in motion their goals to change the nation forever. This was their first dramatic movement. They believed their bold actions would force America to function on the defensive as opposed to the offensive. And they were right. Note the word 'force.' No longer was this generation willing to trust the *institution* to make satisfactory concessions. Empowered by their initial success, they adopted 'force' as the tool to achieve their goals. When I think of 'force' I think of the use of power to intimidate, coerce and/or bully others to submit to distasteful demands. Residue from the events of the *Summer of Love* continue to detract from the values held by the Greatest Generation. The outer layer of the American culture was stripped away. The nation would no longer hold the power and prestige of the past. It would have to resort to defending itself from the criticisms of its youth. Freedom to function offensively was subject to a new order in the hands of novel generations. I think this points to the 'dumbing down' of America. From these writings, see if you can discern a thread that runs through the values, morals, and ethics of the 1940's and those of our current time. I liken this process with the pouring of honey from a jar. First the golden stream coming from the jar is fat, full and sweet. As in winds its way down, the stream becomes a wispy, thin, fine thread barely seen by the naked eye. When the thread becomes invisible it no longer has the properties to be of significance. Thus the convictions held by each generation are all but lost. This has not been by default. It has happened by design.

Early in 1966, in the rippling wake of events surrounding the *Summer of Love*, Larry and I, along with our daughter, Michelle, chose to become a part of a different faith *community*. Even though it was affiliated with the historical church of our parents, it was steeped in seemingly unorthodox visions of what it means to be a believer of Christ. It was the inspiration of a young ambitious visionary who was bound by authenticity and integrity. He conceived an alternative spiritual experience that pointed to the reconciliation and the restoration of faith to those disenchanted with the old paradigms of the church. It was grounded in the scriptures and relevant to the world. I believe today, as I did then, that his profound sense of vision inspired the creation of one of the truest expressions of what it means to be a Christ Follower.

With unashamed courage, the young congregation operated in the warm glow of love and compassion. It offered hope and joy to those who searched for an anchor to steady their lives. Attached to the anchor was an invitation to begin again. The prevailing theme of the church was one that honored and respected all of life. Every participant was encouraged to claim their passions for humanity and to find ways to live through those gifts. If everyone does a little bit of good, those little bits put together can overwhelm the world. Lives were changed because of the little bits of good offered through the *community* of faith. Everyone did their part to carry the light of love and compassion to a torn and ragged world.

When the heart of a *community* is given second priority, the *community* is left vulnerable to the crushing effects of evil. In my seventy-five years, I have witnessed the crumbling of *community* as it succumbs to the evil nature of the *institution*. It is a sad picture.

15.

Change is always on the horizon. That is part of the nature of man and the society surrounding him. Some change is embraced by the *community*. Changes orchestrated for purposes of disrupting the societal order create the pain of loss. Such was the case on November 22, 1963. The change that resulted from the assassination of President Kennedy was instantaneous and hung heavily on the hearts of every American. The nation was shrouded in grief as it processed the ghastly happening and began its slow journey toward the remembering of its identity. America was thrust into a blind race against itself. Little did Larry and I know that we were about to enter a race of our own.

It was 1964. Larry worked for Pan American Petroleum Corporation (Standard of Indiana); they had an office in Columbus, Ohio. In the midst of the nation's grieving the loss of the president, we were transferred to that office. I was hired by the Westerville, Ohio, school system to teach fifth grade. Our immediate geographic displacement was like pushing a fast-forward button in our lives. Sometimes, advancement in the corporate world comes with the trappings of the global world. At this time, one of the trappings of the oil industry was the expectation to re-locate to another area to further the exploration of black crude. In the midst of the oil boom in Kansas, Wyoming, Oklahoma, and other states in the union, moving from one place to another was much like that of military personnel. When it was a frequent happening, it tended to keep a family unsettled and on guard trying to anticipate where or when the next move might happen. Larry and I grew up on farms where our feet were firmly planted in the soil. This arrangement forced us to join the race toward the temporary. As it turned out, it was a blessing that empowered us to grow together as a family.

Our next and last transfer was in 1965. On a hot day in August, an Allied Moving Van led a mini caravan toward Oklahoma City. Larry took our daughter, Michelle, with him in his 1962 Chevrolet. Chuckie, our parakeet, and I brought up the rear in my 1964 Volkswagen Bug. Ohio had been a good place. Now we were going home where new challenges awaited us.

The Oklahoma Education Association (OEA) had placed sanctions on the state for not funding schools properly. That meant schools in the state were advised not to hire teachers from out-of-state. Even though I held an Oklahoma Teaching Certificate, under the mandate, I was denied a position. Most schools followed the imposed action of the OEA. One brave Superintendent of a county school invited me to join his staff as a kindergarten teacher. As a consequence, the position assumed by the OEA paved the way for unions to set up shop in the state educational system. Unions came into being as advocates of teachers. As they grew in numbers they grew in power. In most cases, and in my way of thinking, unions are most appealing to 'bean counters' who view education through the lens of black and white stipulations. They are more concerned with rules and regulations than with the education of children. They are a hindrance rather than an asset. Their focus is on the power of the union to lobby for control that dictates legislation and that pads the coffers of the unions. Today, I think teachers are pawns between the school districts and the unions that hold them. Not a good thing for a free society! This is an example of the *institution* that crushes the *community*. In 1966, sanctions were lifted and I accepted a teaching position in the Putnam City school district.

Across the country, racial unrest was swelling within those who held dreams of catching the golden cord that could offer a brighter future. In and around the town where I grew up, were Native Americans of various tribes. I went to school with kids whose lifestyles included Indian Pow Wows held on the outskirts of town every summer. The family living on the farm near my parents was of the Cherokee Tribe. Legend has it that somewhere in the genealogy of my family is a Cherokee gene. I might question who in Oklahoma doesn't have a gene or two belonging to one tribe or the another? My first awareness that racial issues plagued our nation was when I was in college. Of course, I had learned that President Abraham Lincoln abolished slavery in Washington, D.C. in 1862. In the naivete of my life experiences, I assumed Lincoln's act had 'put-an-end' to the cruel disparaging inequities imposed upon persons of color. That was, until a black choir was asked to perform on the campus of the college I attended. After the concert, my dorm roommate and I pondered where people could spend the night in a town with only one motel. She told me black people could not stay within the city limits after sundown. I was shocked. It never crossed my mind in1956 that black people were treated different from anyone else. I guess I thought that social dilemma was safely tucked away in history.

There were no black people living in or around the rural area of northwest Oklahoma where I grew up. On the other hand, on the ranch in north central Oklahoma near where my father grew up lived a black family. Keep in mind, that was the 1930's. Can you imagine the courage it took for one lone black family to settle in an all-white, rural farm *community* in the thirties? I wish I knew what brought them to the back country along the Cimarron River in Woods County. My father spoke with high regard for Jess Howard. My older siblings remember Jess and Mary Howard. I only know them through the stories told by my father. According to Daddy, Mr. Howard was more than a good neighbor, he was a family friend. Jess and Mary were among the first to visit when my twin brother and I were born. Even though my parents urged them to come close enough to get a good look at us, they approached with caution. They said they were hesitant because they knew we would not have seen a black person and they were afraid we would be frightened. It is so easy to take to your heart people with such sensitivity. During the summer months, Daddy's family held weekly rodeos on their farm. Many times Mr. Howard accepted the challenge of riding a bucking bronco or roping a calf. These were some of the fun times the *community* enjoyed. I guess the recounting of fond stories involving Mr. Howard took precedence over color. Much later, I connected with the reality that Jess and Mary were black. My parents were colorblind. In a time when prejudice ran rampant, it was easy to learn discrimination. I am grateful I didn't learn racial discrimination from my parents.

Televisions in the home had been around for a few years, but we were not privileged to have one. Every Friday night the Cherokee family on the farm next to ours invited us over to watch wrestling on their set. Otherwise, we didn't know much of what went on outside our little corner of the world. Racial incidents were happening in places across the nation. When we moved to Oklahoma City, black people were protesting the right to be served in restaurants. We had a television where we witnessed the sit-ins at Katz Drugstore. Another issue that pricked the nerves of many was that of school integration. To circumvent the demands for children to be bused from white neighborhoods to black neighborhoods and vice versa, schools sprung up in areas outside the city limits. Putnam City was a school established in Warr Acres. Parents withdrew their children from Oklahoma City schools and enrolled them in Putnam City to avoid integration. I am certain "White Flight" occurred in other surrounding districts. All racial issues are born out of bias, bigotry, and fear. Human dignity rests in the hands of those who are compassionate and caring members of society. In writing the script of the Constitution, our forefathers declared that all people were to be entitled to the rights and privileges afforded the total population. It is the right of all to share in the abundance of our nation. I am happy to report that today things have changed dramatically. Persons of all colors may dine in any restaurant, may live in any neighborhood of choice, and may send their children to any school. We've come a long way, but we must continue to persevere until we have erased the lines that would divide us.

There remain those who exploit racism for their own aggrandizement. Some black leaders appear in most any arena for the specific purpose of tossing racism on the table. They continue to pull the scab from the wound to insure healing never happens. If healing were to happen, they would have no place to exercise their divisiveness and might have to get real jobs and quit feeding at the trough of racism. I think with the support of the Constitution and the more recent laws that have been put in place, persons of any color are empowered to pursue their dreams. Bombarding them with images of the victimhood of their ancestors has the effect of holding them in like bondage. I suspect many people of color are weary of the constant comparison between their existence today and that of their ancestors long ago. Some may feel like screaming, "Move on people. This is 2011. I am not my ancestor. Don't rob me of the claim I have made upon my life."

My grandfather was a bootlegger of fine wines, but that doesn't mean I am destined to carry on his or anyone else's indiscretions. He did what he had to do to survive in the harsh years of the 1920's. I honor him by elevating myself to higher aspirations. When you continue to tell a child he is not smart, or not good enough, he will eventually believe the mantra and live a compromised life. The world owes each of us the confirmed message of freedom to grab hold of the golden ring of life then to stand aside as we enjoy the glorious ride toward our dreams. It seems to me there is something sinister in the desire to hold others hostage. I'm not a biblical interpreter, but I think perhaps the story of the lame man lying beside the pool of water might be relevant here. The man explained to Jesus that he was too slow to be the first in the bubbling waters that he believed would heal him. Jesus simply told him to get up, take his mat, and walk. I suggest to you that most of us are, or have been, subjected to situations that cripple us in one way or another. It is imperative that we find someone to bolster our courage to get up, take our cross, and move on down the track. If we never find that someone, we may hold ourselves in bondage forever, never to know the joy of being alive.

About thirty years ago, Mary was a brilliant and successful Loan Officer in a bank. Her husband, Fred, operated a private business. One bright sunny day, Fred had a routine physical check-up. After running several batteries of tests, he was told he had pancreatic cancer. As most persons do, Fred and Mary began the gruesome process of finding someone in the medical field to help them strategize a plan of treatment that would prolong his life. As the medical bills began to mount, they opted to replace their thirty-two hundred square-foot home with one of a lesser size and in a more modest neighborhood. Over a matter of months, Fred's care exhausted their insurance benefits and depleted their bank accounts. They were stripped of all their reserves and forced to depend on the assistance of family. After Fred died, Mary's future was bleak. She tried to go back to work, but grief and depression held her hostage. She had family and *community* support during Fred's illness. After his death, everyone went back to their ordinary lives leaving Mary to search for comfort. It seemed even her body betrayed her. She commenced to have symptoms of all kinds of illnesses. Her knees gave her pain; her stomach hurt; her eyes didn't focus correctly. Before one physical correction was achieved, another would present itself. She discovered personal care and concern in the medical *community*. Her life became a series of doctor appointments and surgeries. Mary became dependent upon pills and procedures. It was easier for her to deal with health issues than it was for her to cope with the losses in her life. She was held hostage by her fear that turning loose of her attack on her body would strip her of any means of comfort. She was in a stuck pattern and could not shake it.

Today, Mary is kinder to herself and to her body. She has found comfort within herself. She is learning to forgive the tragedies of her past and to begin living in the present. Mary connected with persons who had experienced some of the same losses in their lives as she had. The commonality of their circumstances has empowered her to 'look at the glass half full and not the glass half empty.' She takes comfort in knowing that others who share her unique life experiences have not only survived, they have found a renewed source of hope to live.

I suggest to you that multitudes of people are, for whatever reason, stuck in a pattern of bondage of one kind or another. I believe, to a degree, Mary's circumstance mirrors that found in the historical racial inequality and in many other injustices. People who accommodate a neurosis prolong or deny the opportunity to heal. Sometimes their motives are altruistic. Other times they have something to gain by blocking wellness.

As you wander through the events of my life, I hope you will gain a sense of the ebb and flow of evolution in the society of America. At times, there are happenings that threaten to destroy our nation. Other times, when the nation searches for truth in circumstances that cause division and makes responses that have the potential to heal the gaping wound, there is hope toward a brighter future.

Change happens whether we are ready or not. Re-grouping and healing is the result of intensive care. The booming growth of the oil industry, the dilemma of the ever-changing dictates regarding the education of our young, and the perpetual racial 'elephant' in the room, all were issues influencing who our family and the nation would become.

16.

How does a nation reclaim its inherent goodness after it is imprinted with the guilt of ghoulish acts of injustice? How does a nation revive its soul when it has been separated from its original source of life? Perhaps, if we reduce this dilemma to a personal level, we have a greater chance of answering that question with another question. How do you recover from the personal disappointments inflicted upon another in your life? I think many times, as a nation, we try to absolve our sour actions by hurrying on to something else. The operative word here is 'hurrying.' Perhaps that is the way we escape feeling the excruciating pain. We make hasty, short-gap resolutions and hasten on to other issues. Sometimes healing happens when we have the courage to sink into the pain and allow it to scour out the venom of our despair. Hurrying diminishes the effectiveness of who we are as individuals and distracts from the meaningful operations of a nation. Only when we learn to love, truly love, one another and grow in compassion and respect for all of humanity, will healing begin.

I am wary of anyone who uses expediency to deny my opportunity to ruminate on critical issues. On a daily basis, we watch television ads that push us to buy some sort of item that is guaranteed to enhance our lives. We are fervently urged to respond within the next few minutes and we will receive a second one of the same item for just the cost of postage. The message that comes across is, buy now, or you will not have an opportunity later. Every Sunday on our ride to church, commercials on the radio draw attention to all sorts of vitamins (my husband refers to them as 'snake oil') to cure whatever ails you. I once heard of an automobile agency who leaned hard on potential customers. When a customer drove onto the lot, the sales manager closed the gate to the parking area. This tactic was designed to intimidate the person into purchasing a vehicle to gain release from the locked gate. You can almost hear carnival hawkers shouting, "Hurry! Hurry! Step right up and drive away in a shiny, new, luxury car."

Increasingly, we have become a hurry-up society. It is almost like we are in a race to see who can make it through life the fastest. Maybe we are afraid to slow down for fear of missing out on something. On the other hand, if we slow down we might discover the real joy in our journey. What might this say about living in the moment?

I think it is time for us to sit down and let our souls catch up with us. Our nation is comprised of wonderful people, good people, creative people who have at their command what it takes to solve difficult and complex issues. It is good for the government to get out of the way to allow time and freedom for the people to chart their course toward the future. Washington's role is to facilitate and empower the people in their quest for viable answers that protect the rights of all citizens. People deserve to be honored and valued for who they are, not who the government in Washington, D.C. wants them to be.

17.

I continued to teach. By taking night classes and going to summer school, I completed my Masters Degree from Oklahoma City University. Life was simple. Larry had a good job. I was happy teaching first-graders. Our daughter, Michelle, attended the same elementary school where I taught which made mornings a little less stressful. The most important benefit of that arrangement was I could be more involved in Michelle's school experience.

Somehow, the smooth and orderly lifestyle I attempted to create for our family didn't quite work the way I intended. Invariably, the days would become hectic. I wanted to be like June Cleaver of the Leave It To Beaver sitcom with a neat floral print dress covered by a lace trimmed apron, every hair on my head in place, and dinner ready to serve when Larry returned home. Things work out so much better on TV. Come to think of it, I never recall June standing over a hot iron nor scrubbing the commode. Just once, I would have liked to have seen her spill spaghetti sauce down the front of her lovely dress just minutes before her guests arrived. Of course her delightful little apron would have protected her lovely little dress. How did she manage her days without getting frustrated and frantic? Yes, I know the difference between reality and fantasy. There were days I didn't even like June Cleaver. I have always desired time to ponder and reflect. For working mothers that seems to be a rarity, if not totally out of reach. I was happily married and had a beautiful child, but occasionally it felt as though I was being hurled through time and space. Larry's mother used to talk of how with each year time escaped faster. She was right. I don't want time to stand still, but I would like it to slow to a more comfortable pace. My competition with June Cleaver hastened as the beating drums of time demanded I dance faster to stay ahead. In the spring of 1972, Michelle asked me to make her a dress for a special occasion. My response went something like this, "I don't have time to make a dress." Those words stung my conscience. I was so busy taking care of other people's children, I had little time or energy to fulfill the needs of my own child. The following day I requested and submitted a resignation form. The Principal said he would hold the form as he was certain I would re-think my action. I knew without a doubt that my decision was right.

18.

July 20th, 1969, Neil Armstrong and Buz Aldren landed Apollo 11 in the Sea of Tranquility on the moon. I was confined to a hospital room after having had minor surgery. Sedation clouded my memory, but I still hear Neil Armstrong say, 'The Eagle Has Landed.' If that doesn't put a lump in your throat, I don't know what will. It makes me think of Rita Cosby's book 'Quiet Hero.' She tells of her father's capture and imprisonment in a concentration camp in Germany. It was near the end of World War II when word began to circulate through the camp that the Americans were coming to rescue them. Rita recounts her father's brave escape from the camp and his tireless, seemingly endless walk to the Americans. He told Rita of his profound relief when he reached the other side of the river lined by U.S. soldiers. How glorious it must have been to be greeted by American soldiers, thanking them for being saved and the assurance that Rita's father and his fellow captives would be cared for. I urge you to read Rita's book. Her father's story is compelling. Incidentally, Rita's father was a part of an activist group of young people called 'The Young Eagles.' The Eagle Has Landed! Pride in our nation comes so easy when you learn the stories of those who have been blessed by the sacrifices young men and women have made in the battle for freedom.

For anyone who might not know, the eagle is a bird characterized by its powerful build, broad wing span, fast flight, and keen eyesight and it symbolizes all that and more to the United States.

The mission to the moon was a glorious achievement. President Kennedy set the space program in place with a goal of reaching the moon before the end of the 1960's. The landing in July 1969, was a victory to the U.S. in the Cold War space race with the Soviets.

America is great and powerful. It operates with a profound sense of greatness. I pray we never lose sight of the heroic acts of our nation. They set us apart from other nations. Remember who we are and what we stand for - peace and freedom for all. It is in our remembering that we find the vision and courage to become more than we ever dreamed we could be. In the seclusion of our souls we come to terms with, and absolve ourselves of, the burdens of guilt by omission or co-mission that plague our hearts.

In a speech President Reagan said, "The poet called Miss Liberty's torch, 'the lamp beside the golden door.' Well, that was the entrance to America, and it still is. The glistening hope of that lamp is still ours. Every promise, every opportunity is still golden in this land. And through that golden door our children can walk into tomorrow with the knowledge that no one can be denied the promise that is America. Her heart is full; her torch is still golden, her future bright. She has arms big enough to comfort and strong enough to support, for the strength in her arms is the strength of her people. She will carry on in the eighties unafraid, unashamed, and unsurpassed. In this springtime of hope, some lights seem eternal; America's is."

19.

With his wife, Pat, by his side President Richard Milhous Nixon, the thirty-seventh president of the United States from 1969 to 1974, turned in the door of the presidential helicopter to wave a final goodbye to those standing on the tarmac. On August 9th, 1974, President Nixon stepped down from office amidst rumors of probable impeachment because of a political scandal involving a break-in to the Democratic National Committee headquarters at the Watergate office complex. Nixon was believed to have been party to the improprieties leading to the break-in. With memories of the assassination of President John F. Kennedy still fresh in the minds of the nation, an impeachment would have driven another nail in the heart of America. It was another unbelievable happening that shrouded the nation with shame and sadness. Nixon's main offense was not telling the truth when the events happened. The nation would have forgiven him just as it did President Clinton at the time of his indiscretions. I believe President Nixon's most endangering transgression was his act of infecting America with the toxicity of deceitfulness. His actions brought disgrace upon himself and upon America. It changed the politics of Washington and of America. It empowered the corruption of the news media in its penchant to report the news with a biased and sensational agenda. Shame on the media for using deception and distortion to taint the hearts and minds of the people. Traces of Mr. Nixon's unscrupulous behavior remain and some say are exhibited in our current administration.

Minutes after the helicopter lift-off on the morning of August 9th, 1974, Vice President Gerald Ford was sworn into office as the thirty-eighth president of the United States to fill the gaping hole of the Presidency. At the swearing in, Ford commented: "I assume the Presidency under extraordinary circumstances.... This is an hour of history that troubles our minds and hurts our hearts." He had been in Congress before he was chosen Nixon's Vice President. Ford was the flip-side of Nixon. He had a steady, mild demeanor. He was unashamedly honest and unafraid of exposing his vulnerabilities. I don't remember eventful changes he made to political policies during his tenure. President Ford believed curbing Government intervention and spending as a means of solving the problems of American society, would bring a better life for all Americans. The U.S. could benefit from revisiting

Ford's beliefs. I believe Ford's greatest gift to a wounded America was a time to stand still and heal. According to some, "Sometimes standing still is the best move you can make." Gerald Ford was what the nation needed at that time. An aura of authenticity and dignity surrounded First Lady, Betty Ford. She had been a dancer and a fashion coordinator before becoming the wife of ex-football hero, Gerald Ford. She accepted the challenges of the wife of a politician with grace and self-confidence. During their time in the White House, Betty Ford underwent radical surgery for breast cancer and reassured many troubled women by discussing her ordeal openly. She became a compassionate friend to those who shared her agonizing circumstance. The social environment in Washington is demanding. As a result, Betty Ford shared details of her dependency on prescription drugs and alcohol. She created the Betty Ford Center for the treatment of this problem.

I remember the day of Nixon's helicopter departure from Washington with sadness and with a glimmer of hope. There is pain in witnessing the life-blood of one being spilled on the tarmac of life. In America, there remains hope in the foresight of the creators of our constitution who built in special provisions for the installation of a reserve leader. I am grateful to live in a democratic nation where laws are implemented to govern equitably and facilitate a sense of order. Sad to say, those laws are not always followed, but they are there.

Every wounding blow to the nation interrupts the rhythm of it's life and forces the people into a frightful panic diminishing their ability to create meaningful responses. Every act of indiscretion chips away the goodness of who we are.

20.

James Earl Carter, a genteel southerner from the state of Georgia, was inaugurated as the thirty-ninth President of the United States in 1977. He was a former governor of the 'Peach State.' After his father died, Mr. Carter resumed the processing operations of his peanut plantation. President Carter was a soft-spoken gentleman who wore an easy smile and had a glint in his kind eyes. He was a good man, a good man. He aspired to make government "competent and compassionate," and responsive to the social concerns of the nation. Many of his ideals seemed euphoric and unrealistic for the time. With little experience in the inner workings of Washington, his presidency was wrought with disappointment. Congress blocked many of his ideas.

President Carter and his wife, Rosalynn, were devout Christians and maintained strong ties with their family and the Baptist church. They spoke with the slow, warm drawl characteristic of the South. They blessed the White House with southern charm and hospitality. Rosalynn used Carter's boyhood name, Jimmy, in referencing him. Rosalynn and Jimmy were humanitarians and brought to the surface issues involving social justice and human rights. After leaving office, they became involved in Habitat For Humanity. They never shirked from being involved with their resources and with their physical labor. Whatever might be said about Jimmy Carter, I believe he modeled the Presidency after his values and respect for the nation and the people. He was honest, moral, ethical, and good. The image he presented to the nation gave our children a view of the attributes of a person who lived with authenticity.

Many times following his years as President, Carter was called upon to arbitrate controversial humanitarian issues between nations. He was presented the Nobel Peace Award for his efforts in working toward peace.

It is sad when good men go to Washington with hopes of making a positive difference and find themselves seduced into sacrificing their principles for the sake of the political party. I wonder if part of President Carter's ineffectiveness in Washington stems from the gap between politics and ethics. He went to Washington to bring about a kinder, gentler, authentic, and trust-worthy nation. I wrote the following paragraph in February of 2006.

I read Jimmy Carter's book, "Our Endangered Values." It brings to awareness some of the values we have come to call truths in our nation. Jimmy Carter is a good man. I thank him for his compassionate gift of awareness. Mr. Carter was a President who came into office with hopes and dreams of making a difference in how our nation values human life. He was a man whose values were sound. Our values are endangered. A tragedy happened in February of 2006 as the world watched Mr. Carter surrender his soul to partisan politics. At the services honoring Coretta Scott King, Mr. Carter chose to use his time at the podium to criticize current political issues. I believe his criticisms of President George W. Bush were shameful and despicable. In his efforts to fulfill his political agenda, I believe he sent a message to the world that it is okay to forfeit the honoring of basic values if the political atmosphere requires it. To destroy the reverence and respect for Mrs. King and her family was to sacrifice the endangered value of regard for human life. In my opinion, this was a blatant example of a good man influenced to shine his light on the negative rather than on what is positive and honorable. The funeral of Coretta King was neither about President Bush nor his politics. It was about remembering the gentle spirit of a woman who made a difference in the life of every American. Opinion of some may mourn Mr. Carter's loss of reverence, honor, and respect because his loss is a loss for each of us. A torch may have been dropped that would have helped light the way toward compassion, goodness, integrity, and decency.

There is no substitute for honor and discretion.

21.

On January 20, 1981, Ronald Reagan was inaugurated as the fortieth President of the United States. I would characterize him as a President who inspired the *community* to hope. He gave more than lip-service to his enthusiasm toward preserving the greatness of America. He empowered the people. Mr. Reagan had been the governor of California. Before that, he had been a movie actor. Nancy, his wife and the First Lady, had previously appeared on the screen. She held strong influence over the President. I remember watching Ronald Reagan in movies of the old West. With eyes that twinkled with delight, an easy smile, and wisdom that offered hope, he drew people into his confidence. When he became President he embraced the realities of that position and left the fantasies of the actor on the stage. As an actor, he developed the art of speaking with confident resolve. The ambiance surrounding Reagan's straightforward presence and his words of substance and depth were his products of believability. When he stood before the cameras he could be counted on to offer clear succinct views of how things were in the nation.

Reagan once said, "We who live in free market societies believe that growth, prosperity, and ultimately, human fulfillment are created from the bottom up, not the government down. Only when the human spirit is allowed to invent and create, only when individuals are given a personal stake in deciding economic policies and benefitting from their success - only then can societies remain economically alive, dynamic, progressive, and free. Trust the people. This is the one irrefutable lesson of the entire postwar period contradicting the notion that rigid government controls are essential to economic development." As far as I am concerned, his words say it all in understanding the role *institution* should play in supporting the *community*. We need to emblazon these words on our foreheads to help us maintain a clear vision of who we are as a society. With President Reagan, everything was clear cut. He made most Americans feel safe.

Many in the world remember his command: "Mr. Gorbachev, open this gate! Mr. Gorbachev, tear down this wall!" Reagan was a uniting President.

To me, his most profound statement was: "If we lose freedom here, there is no place to escape to." This statement revealed his understanding about the significance of the U.S. in relation to the rest of the world. Reagan was more than an actor or a

President. He was a true Statesman. In 1992, he declared his hope for a kind legacy when he said: "Whatever else history may say about me when I'm gone, I hope it will record that I appealed to your best hopes, not your worst fears, to your confidence rather than your doubts. My dream is that you will travel the road ahead with liberty's lamp guiding your steps and opportunity's arm steadying your way. My fondest hope for each one of you—and especially for the young people here—is that you will love your country, not for her power or wealth, but for her selflessness and her idealism. May each of you have the heart to conceive, the understanding to direct, and the hand to execute works that will make the world a little better for your having been here. May all of you as Americans never forget your heroic origins, never fail to seek divine guidance and never lose your natural, God-given optimism. And finally, my fellow Americans, may every dawn be a great new beginning for America and every evening bring us closer to that shining city upon a hill." He embraced the *community* of America and used his gifts to heighten and repair the image of the nation.

Reagan affirmed the power in the strengths of our nation when he said, "Only our deep moral values and our strong social *institutions* can hold back the jungle and restrain the darker impulses of nature."

Thank you, Mr. President, for believing in the *community* of America and blessing it with vision and wisdom.

22.

For several months in 1989, Iraq, under the leadership of Saddam Hussein, had been making overtures toward a take-over of Kuwait. On January 16, 1991, a U.S. led coalition of forces authorized by the United Nations made an unexpected invasion of Iraq. I remember sitting on the end of my bed as I watched the initial invasion. Journalists imbedded with the military gave us a front row seat to witness war, the kind that wounds and kills. Television has a way of drawing each of us in to witness the horrifying blow-by-blow effects of everything and war is no exception. What were the feelings of the young men and women who were asked to carry out this mission? I feel certain fear was cloaked in their bones. And what about the ordinary innocent citizens of Kuwait? How could they protect themselves from bombs rushing toward the earth? Rarely before has our nation been subjected to the pain of invading another country. I have mixed feelings toward inviting the world to witness the reprimands of war. It had been the policy of America to remain neutral when other nations had disagreements. On the other hand, how does the world stand idly by as smaller nations are viciously stripped of their independence to be held hostage by cruel dictators? I saw this as an instance when our nation sacrificed the convictions of our hearts to follow the consensus of the United Nations. In a nation with little or no tolerance for the infliction of pain on others, I have no answers, but I hope someday we take time to sit down and figure them out. How do we learn to behave responsibly? How does a nation with the power to save, take a few steps back when called to take sides in the bickering of other nations? What I do believe is that America sacrifices a bit of its innate goodness when it interacts with the evilness of the world. So what does that say about the nature of our responses? That is something we must think about.

The war ended February 28, 1991, just 43 days after it began and when Kuwait was liberated from the clutches of the Iraqi dictatorship. George Herbert Walker Bush, the forty-first President of the United States between 1989 and 1993, was a quiet Texan. He was responsible for rescuing Kuwait from an Iraqi take-over. He referred to the invasion of Iraq as Desert Storm. President George H. Bush and the First Lady, Barbara, were well thought of. Barbara Bush was afforded a warm greeting by the nation. She referred to herself as "everybody's grandmother." She was enshrouded by a gentle softness, white hair, relaxed manner, and keen wit. Barbara Bush felt the people liked her because "I'm fair and I like children and I adore my husband." People were drawn to her in friendship.

Children are the most important part of any circumstance in life. Many times they are left out of the equation of who we are. Some times their presence is negated. It was refreshing to hear the First Lady express her fondness for children.

23.

I have presented clues characteristic of the American culture between 1936 and 2011 as evidence that reflects the deterioration of attitudes, morés, social order, and political climate framing my life.

There was a time when government (*institution*) was pro-*community*. Presidents swore on a bible to make the welfare of the nation their primary goal. Yes, leaders committed violations of ethics, but they were in the minority and were held accountable. Today, the violations of leaders are more pervasive. We have basked in the glory of scientific achievements and in the age of technology. The eagle, a powerful force, has landed. America continues to be on the forefront of new discoveries that enhance the quality of life for all its citizens and those of others around the globe. Now, the vibrant life of the greatest nation of all time lives in a shameful era of terror. It began with occasional violent acts against the U.S. and has escalated to more frequent and aggressive invasions. The bombing of the World Trade Center buildings on September 11, 2011 (9/11) was a dramatic insult to the US and tarnished our unrelenting commitment to freedom for all. Since that time the nation has scrambled for ways to thwart and protect the *community* of America. It is incomprehensible that there are those who would cross our shores for the purpose of destroying the innocence of the nation. Most people are humbled by their first glimpse of the Statute of Liberty in the New York Harbor. Lady Liberty lures the oppressed and the weary into the world of freedom. In these last ten years following 9/11, we have seen a dramatic shift in the behavior of our nation - once a confident nation in its efforts toward securing peace in the world and now a nation that operates out of self-doubt ignited by criticisms and accusations.

Recently some Islamists hoped to erect a mosque near the site of the World Trade Center's devastation. Many citizens carrying the scars of 9/11 felt this was thoughtless and insensitive! As a nation embracing freedom for all, we set few limits on those coming here. What was once a few peaceful Islamic people living in our midst has become thousands and many of those who came for freedom are being held hostage by radicals within their ranks. As we continue to diminish the existence of Christianity in our society, we sometimes hand the keys of our faith to others. Does it make any sense to expect radicals, who have only known violence, to be in charge of preserving freedom? I think this will be a perpetual problem until the moral, ethical, law-abiding Islamists outwardly exhibit an appreciation for and defense of the values and morals in this country. If freedom is their reason for coming here, it doesn't make any sense to me that their goal would be to re-create the distresses of where they came from. When persons of any origin, come here with the intention of replicating their homeland, I believe they come for the wrong reasons. Many times that agenda is not in the best interest of preserving the rights and privileges of America. Islamic people, who want to be Americans, should indicate they are sincere in presenting themselves as individuals who hold moral and ethical values. If they come here seeking a better way of life, they will need to lay aside that which caused them angst in their homeland and adopt an open and honest regard for human life.

When good, self-respecting Islamic people speak up in the face of terrorism perpetrated by radicals of their faith, they are a part of the solution that will keep freedom alive. To remain silent makes them a part of the problem that spreads the cancerous venom of deception, hatred, and revenge which denies freedom. I believe that much like our troubled educational system, the re-visioning of the culture of their nations will only happen from the ground up, from infancy into adulthood. Morals, ethics, and respectful attitudes are born in the compassions of the soul. It is time for Islamists to step forward to claim their rightful identity as it has been stolen by radicals who twist Islamic beliefs and laws to justify terroristic behavior.

The Eagle landed to bring freedom to all. America has freedom as its mantra. It continues to use its resources (economic and human manpower in the trenches) to assist other nations in their quest to create a more peaceful society.

Often the United States is referred to as the 'melting pot' of the world. This characterizes who we are as a nation. Multiplicity is the strength of America.

Today immigration seems to be mushrooming faster than those coming here can be assimilated. The red tape surrounding application for citizenship appears complicated and unwieldy. In desperation, many times those whose countries border ours by-pass regulations and enter illegally. Today there is a large Hispanic population in America. Most are hardworking law abiding citizens. Many are illegal immigrants who place a major economic burden on the nation.

During and following the Vietnam War, many Asians migrated to the US. Those I have known are incredibly resilient people who create economic opportunities and take pride in being responsible and productive citizens. Across the nation there are pockets of Asian communities. Many beautify declining neighborhoods. In my years of teaching, I have known Asian parents who take parenting seriously and who expect their children to behave appropriately and perform well academically. For a few years, I volunteered at a school for homeless children. In my time there, I did not see one Asian child who was homeless. Asian families take care of each other.

In every state in the union, there is a large population of native American Indians. They are among the first inhabitants of the nation. Multitudes of tribes are located across America. In western Oklahoma, I lived in the midst of these warm, gentle, peace-loving people. Contrary to what some might believe, native Americans are quiet, laid back people who honor their heritage. Each year at the Red Earth

Celebration they share traditions of native dress, tribal dances, intricate and elaborate artistry. Theirs is a culture rich in history and folklore. The story below is a legend. I say legend because I can neither prove nor disprove its authenticity.

'An air of sacredness hung over her as she made her way through the mountains of North Carolina. The gentle rhythmic clip clop of her paint pony could be heard above the stillness of the tall pines. Her serene buckskin clothed body staunch with resignation straddled the bareback of her steed while her long raven braid swayed with indifference to his cadence. Her right hand clutched the mane of her horse to give directions; her left hand held a small bundle wrapped in swaddling clothes.

She was Cherokee but the bundle she carried was 'half breed.' It was 1837 and the United States government was relocating her tribe. Some were sent to Kentucky, some to Ohio, and some as far away as Oklahoma. Those with 'half breed' were ordered to choose between their native tribe, the white family of their offspring, or a life of solitude in the mountains. Choosing to stay with the Cherokees was a mandate to forfeit her child. To keep her child meant permanent rejection from her native tribe and all it's rights. For herself and her child she chose to unite with the white family of her child. In a real sense that choice caused her to be sent away without protection or means of survival. Still she rode with confidence and determination as she made her way toward the unknown world of the white man.

Years later she would realize the blessing of her choice. In 1837 the Cherokee Tribe was sent on one of the saddest journeys recorded in the history of our country. Removed from their territory and herded across the nation like the buffalo they hunted, the gentle, innocent red men were stripped of their pride and courage. They were forced to walk some two hundred grueling days to what was to be a promised territory but to what turned out to be a barren land with little resources for survival. Many died along the way. The bloodstained trail of the Cherokee Nation is known as the Trail of Tears.

Legend has it that the courageous young Cherokee maiden, who was sent away from her tribe, was my great great grandmother. Fable or fiction, I am warmed by the story and I am honored by the thought that the blood of my native American ancestors flows through my veins.'

America is a nation rich in cultural diversity. Spiritual by nature, Native Americans are more prone to 'walk gently upon the earth and run with their souls.'

We are all immigrants and responsible caring immigrants are and always have been the fiber and soul of our great nation.

24.

In 1993, William Clinton became the forty-second President of the United States. Hillary Clinton became the First Lady. She was very involved in many facets of the political environment in Washington. President Clinton was a young man from Hope, Arkansas. His charming and charismatic personality endeared him to many. It was believed he was the man 'for the people.' Clinton enjoyed the aura that surrounded his Presidency. As with many leaders, rumors of back-door dealings hung in the air. During his time in office, the U.S. is said to have enjoyed more peace and economic well-being than at any time in history. Low unemployment rate, low inflation, high home ownership, drop in crime rates, and reduced welfare rolls account for much of his success. He proposed a balanced budget and called for an initiative to end racial discrimination. Clinton failed at healthcare reform. He sought legislation to upgrade education, to protect jobs of parents who must care for sick children, to restrict handgun sales, and to strengthen environmental regulations.

A shadow was cast on the Clinton Presidency when he had a less than honorable relationship with a young woman on his staff. He stood before cameras in the White House and declared to the nation that he did not have a relationship with her. That was clearly not true. (How can we expect to create a world with morals and conscience when the President is dishonest?) The House of Representatives voted for his impeachment. The Senate voted it down. As I recall few or no Democrats in the Senate crossed party lines to declare Clinton's guilt. This was the first time in my life to witness the demoralization of members of Congress through the blatant denial of truth. A shadow of disgrace was cast on the President and on the nation. And the faith of the nation took another blow to the chin.

Mr. Clinton has been known to fall in the ditch of verbal disasters. On July 2, 2010, President Clinton eulogized Senator Robert C. Byrd, the Senator from West Virginia. He shared the events surrounding Byrd's arrival on the political stage. He made a statement about newspapers making comments about Byrd once having a fleeting association with the Ku Klux Klan. Clinton reasoned that Byrd was just a country boy from the hills of West Virginia and was just trying to get elected. He indicated Byrd spent the remainder of his life making amends and that is what a good person does.

One might interpret that to mean it is acceptable to participate in clandestine activities if it is for the good of getting elected. Surely, Mr. Clinton had knowledge of the hellacious murders of black people by the Klan. It is flippant and shameful to rationalize wrong as right. It is no wonder our young are confused in discerning what is right from that which is not right. I am sad for Mr. Clinton's failure to honor those who suffered the loss of life at the hands of criminals. I believe this is another instance when good men use skewed logic to justify evil.

Despite Mr. Clinton's lapse in judgment, I believe he is an intelligent person. When duty called, he drew on the innate goodness of his soul to make a difference. Following the bombing of the Alfred P. Murrah Federal Building in Oklahoma City on April 19, 1995, President Clinton and First Lady, Hillary, attended a memorial service honoring those who died in the blast. Their presence was warm and compassionate and reverent. They did not use the moment as a political event. They simply came to mourn with us. That day they brought dignity and respect to the leadership of the *institution* of our government. It was comforting to know the President of the United States could call forth values of decency and dignity in a time of tragedy. Mr. Clinton honored the dictates of the Presidency.

Today, Mr. Clinton enjoys a popularity rating greater than the sitting president. He has been generous in using his Presidential role to further humanitarian efforts. I believe Clinton's greatest gift to the nation was his passion and patriotism. I trusted his warm heart. It is hard not to embrace, at some level, a President who smiles more than he frowns and appears to be happy rather than angry. He trusted in the goodness of the American people. Whether you liked Clinton or not, the ambiance around his presence lifted the spirits of the nation. It takes more trust and faith to counter the guilt imposed at other times in our history.

I can't help but wonder if in the recesses of Mr. Clinton's soul there was a momentary disconnect from decency that will plague him the remainder of his life.

25.

Contrast the America of the forties with the one of the year two thousand one. In the forties, America operated under a policy of neutrality which meant not getting involved with the affairs of other nations. In two thousand one, the policy of neutrality once embraced by our nation became extinct. Foreign terrorists struck down the innocence of the U.S. and became an overriding theme of the nation.

Terrorism has been a way of life in many countries especially those in the Middle East. In America, it was incomprehensible to believe someone would intentionally create explosives to kill others. The first act of terrorism on our soil occurred on February 26, 1992. A bomb was detonated under the North Tower of the World Trade Center in New York City. I suspect that was seen as a one-time deed carried out by a hostile person. Little did we know that it would be a precursor to more destructive acts.

The morning of April 19, 1995, I was sitting in the lower level of our church fifteen miles away from downtown Oklahoma City when the building shook from a frightful blast. It sounded much like the sonic boom of an aircraft. Someone in a nearby office rushed to turn on the television. Through the years, America's responses to the evils of the world have been beyond our borders. All that changed when terrorism struck at the heartland of the nation.

On the night of April 18, 1995, Timothy McVeigh and Terry Nichols assembled a bomb near the Dreamland Motel in Junction City, Kansas. They packed it in a Ryder rental truck and in the early morning hours of April 19th, McVeigh drove the truck to Oklahoma City. After parking it in front of the Alfred P. Murrah Federal Building, he walked the few blocks to a vehicle waiting for him. At exactly 9:02AM, the bomb detonated killing one hundred sixty-eight people and injuring many others. It was a horrifying scene. Men, women, and children were blown apart and crushed in the rubble of the building. Timothy McVeigh was said to have been an anti-militia sympathizer angry at the government for the events at Ruby Ridge and Waco, Texas. He was apprehended ninety minutes after the attack driving up Interstate thirty-five near Perry, Oklahoma. He was driving without a license and unlawfully carrying a firearm.

In the midst of the pain and the horror, the people of Oklahoma City poured out of their places of comfort and organized a rescue effort like none other. In a heartbeat, first aid arrived on the scene. Doctors, nurses, firemen, ministers, rescue agencies, neighbors, families, and friends were there to assist the wounded and to comfort the brokenhearted. Housewives prepared dozens of sandwiches in their kitchens for the rescue workers. Food suppliers donated food. Churches set up rescue places complete with food, water, and cots for family members waiting word of their loved one. Less than an hour after it happened, Larry, who is a Care Chaplain, was able to make his way through the emergency traffic to help. Rescue people came from all over the state and the United States. I have always been proud of Oklahomans and their respect for the human dignity of all. On this day in April, my heart swelled with pride. No one thought to wait for FEMA (Federal Emergency Management Agency) to come to the rescue. And those whose infirmities prevented them from coming to the site prayed. Prayer was on the breath of every person. Faith was restored in human compassion and decency. If you ever want to see what great people look like, come to Oklahoma and you will see goodness splattered everywhere. Don't forget to visit the beautiful memorial erected in honor of those who gave their lives. To think, one of our own committed this terrible act. What a shame! Timothy McVeigh was tried, found guilty, and executed by lethal injection. As his accessory, Terry Nichols was sentenced to, and is serving, life in prison.

Authorities believed Timothy McVeigh's motive was revenge for the government's actions at Ruby Ridge and The Branch Dividian's compound in Waco, Texas.

Ruby Ridge involved the U.S. Secret Service 1985 investigation of allegations that Randy Weaver, purportedly associated with a white supremacist group, had made threats against the President and other government and law enforcement officials. Efforts to arrest Weaver, his family, and a friend resulted in the deaths of a deputy marshall and Weaver's wife and son.

At trial, the court criticized the FBI for its failure to produce discovering materials and obeying orders of the court. A jury acquitted Weaver and his friend of the murder of the deputy and the significant remaining charges. Weaver was released from incarceration in December 1993. This event was a tragedy that left a scar on our indomitable nation.

David Koresh who thought himself to be an angel and an agent of God, was the leader of the Branch Dividians in Waco, Texas. As a charismatic leader of the cult of Christianity, he gathered many followers into Mount Carmel, a communal compound. When Koresh took control of the Waco Branch of Dividians, he annulled the marriages of his followers and claimed exclusive right of marriage for himself. Several followers left the group. A former follower told authorities that Koresh beat the children until they were bruised and bleeding. Social workers investigated but could never confirm the allegations.

The Davidians buried an old school bus to serve as a bunker and a place to stockpile food and ammunition. A showdown came when government agents attempted to arrest Koresh on charges of illegal firearms and explosives. Gunfire erupted. The FBI and Koresh tried to negotiate a reasonable settlement. They were at a standoff for fifty-one days. Operating in the fear that Koresh would lead his followers to a mass suicide, the Davidians were warned of an eminent government invasion. At noon on April 19, 1993, fires started in the compound. Nine Davidians fled. Koresh and seventy-six followers, men, women, and children perished in the flames.

Another sad incident that wounded the soul of America.

Then, there was the horrendous disaster of 9/11. It was the first major terrorist attack on the U.S. soil. On September 11, 2001, airplanes commanded by terriorists flew kamikaze missions into the two World Trade Center towers in New York City killing nearly three thousand people. Another such plane made its way toward the nation's capitol destroying part of the Pentagon. A plane destined to strike the White House was thwarted by the pilot and passengers. It crashed in a field in Pennsylvania leaving no survivors. It was the most paralyzing day I have ever known in our nation. Al-Qaeda terrorists led by Osama bin Laden took credit for this dastardly deed. It was an act much like the bombing of Pearl Harbor in 1941. With the deterioration of behaviors from kind and thoughtful to angry and deadly, America was forced to take a stand. Any remnants of neutrality were taken off the negotiating table. President George W. Bush, the forty-third President, proclaimed America would take a stand against those who perpetrated this heinous and cruel act of aggression upon the nation. This event tended to unite the nation and the world in the fight against terrorism and those who would ignite fear around the globe.

26.

George Walker Bush, son of President George Herbert Walker Bush, was inaugurated the forty-third President on January 20, 2001. On September 11, 2001, he and the First Lady, Laura Bush, were participating in a school event in Florida promoting the joy of learning to read, when he was made aware of the brazen acts of terrorists against our nation. His presidency will be forever marked by 9/11 and the Iraq War.

For some time, there had been a growing concern in the middle east regarding the suspicion that Iraq was creating and harboring weapons of mass destruction (WMD's.) Saddam Hussein held neighboring countries hostage with the threat of using his arsenal of deadly weapons to gain dominance in the area. His earlier attempt to take over Kuwait had been thwarted. The United Nations had reprimanded him on numerous occasions. Iraq was placed under sanctions of all kinds. Saddam persisted. I believe his dictatorship was much like that of Hitler in World War II. He committed cruelties upon his own people that the civilized world found difficult to comprehend. Under the direction of the U.N., Iraq was ordered to allow inspections of the silos housing his military weapons. Saddam denied access to the inspectors.

Then there was the 9/11 attack by the Al-Qaeda on America. It was believed that Iraq was a safe haven for training members of the Al-Qaeda.

On March 3, 2003, a military campaign (Operation New Dawn) comprised of multinational forces led by troops from the U.S. and the United Kingdom invaded Iraq. I did not agree with the decision to go to war, but I didn't have another idea for dealing with an incorrigible nation that refused to cooperate with the regulations of the U.N.

The search for WMD's was futile. I believe Saddam Hussein had the weapons, but when an invasion was eminent he transported them across his borders to countries sympathetic to his cause. Those countries may have acquiesced in fear. Hussein went into hiding, but was captured by U.S. military forces. He was tried in an Iraqi court, was found guilty, and was executed.

The Iraq War and 9/11 became President George W. Bush's cross to bear. At this point, I am obliged to remind readers that I am the author. These are my beliefs and perceptions regarding the events and personalities of this time. My opinions are mine and as such, are not up for debate. So don't even entertain it. If you do not agree, I encourage you to write your version.

Now, to President Bush. First of all, it is my belief he is a good man who, in campaigning for the role of leader of a free nation, did not bargain for these deplorable circumstances. Secondly, I believe George W. Bush has a good heart. The twinkle in his eyes and the causal gestures of his body, speak of his passion for America and its concerns. His soft, warm heart is a quality we hope to have in a President. I believe the United States is greater than any one President. Contributions and errors are the products of everyone who sits in the Oval office. Did he make mistakes? Yes, he made errors of judgment - errors without malice, but errors nonetheless. The price of remorse is high. Three o'clock in the morning is when most of us wrestle with the pain of erroneous deeds committed the previous day. Can you begin to imagine the weight of errors made in the oval office of this great nation? Well, that was George Bush's plight.

If you have gotten this far in reading these pages, you know my thoughts on the erosion of the nation's sense of itself. In the last seventy years, we've done a fast slide down from attitudes of greatness following World War II to those of impotency today. We have witnessed the decline of regard for human life. America, once a nation marked by its goodness, now a nation tainted with shades of evilness. We've offered our goodness to nations who don't know the meaning of gratitude. In exchange, we have become colored by their hostilities. Once we were a happy, genial nation; now we are a divided, angry nation.

We have come to own the shame and guilt of our past actions, but we haven't found a way to forgive ourselves. We offer money and assistance, but that doesn't satisfy the debt.

The ill regard for the person of George W. Bush has been despicable. Never before have I known some people of the United States of America to exhibit such profound cruelty toward another human being. How can being demeaning and hurtful toward another be acts of goodness? During the Bush Presidency, the media conducted a shameful campaign against the man in the oval office. They carried the evil chants to crucify this man whose greatest fault was in believing he could make a positive difference. Our current leader shamelessly continues to thrown stones of torture at President Bush. Evil happens when ordinary men surrender their souls to selfish ambitions. Mr. Bush carried a torch toward a softer, gentler nation, but with the devil in the media on his back, it wasn't possible. In my opinion, the current President has used the vulnerabilities of George Bush to divert blame from where blame belongs. This is beyond shameful! The media and the government was ruthless in setting up roadblocks to prevent the success of President Bush's policies. They were like arsonists surrounding a stalwart building and fueling the fires of twisted truths and deceptions. Ringing across the nation were echoes of the historic cries, "Crucify him. Crucify him." Cruelty and shame marked the country and cloaked it in dishonor. Where were the people of honor? To be sure, they were not in the White House nor on the nightly news. The media has incited more shame and disgrace on our nation than has ever been known before.

I apologize to you Mister President George W. Bush. I long for your warmer, gentler nation. And I pray for the return of joy to your life.

One thing is certain, President George W. Bush gifted the nation with one of the most gracious First Ladies of my lifetime. The President said on many occasions that Laura was the best thing that ever happened to him. She was a warm and magnanimous representative of the American people, a teacher, and a librarian. She made literacy a global issue. Laura Bush probably championed more global causes than any other First Lady since Eleanor Roosevelt.

27.

When you calculate the cumulative effects of the intentional creation of crisis to change the world, the disgrace of the impending impeachment of two Presidents, the assassination of President Kennedy, the inequality of racism, and the perpetual loss of morals and ethics, it is easy to understand how we have evolved as a nation running without a soul. Today, we have arrived at a place where the Baby Boomers hold the keys to the *institution*. This is a very scary place for our nation.

Earlier I wrote of a charismatic figure who led Germany into the ruins of the Holocaust. Ronald Reagan was a charismatic president who captured the respect of many. He entered with the fanfare of an actor who knew his part and he played it to the theater. I wrote about the charisma of President Clinton who embraced good in many respects, but also manipulated others behind the scenes. Now, another person of charisma has surfaced. Unfortunately, he has lost the respect of many in the nation.

In that vein of thought, I wrote that the purpose of government is two-fold. First, it is to nurture optimism and hope in man's eternal search for new visions of the future. Second, it is to assist in the creation of an *institution* of structures and laws that support the societal needs of the *community* it serves. In a democratic society, the leader of the *institution* of government is the President. I intend for readers to interpret this to say that the role of the President is to inspire and facilitate the desires and wishes of the *community*.

Barack Obama was born on August 4, 1961. On January 20, 2009, he became the forty-fourth President of the *institution* of the government of the United States. He entered the political scene as a person with a charismatic personality and charismatic rhetoric. As a candidate, he described his work experience as that of a *Community* Organizer in Chicago, Illinois. Perhaps in that role he exploited those who believed they were victims of the inequities of society. Instead of inspiring the *community* to reach for goals that would enhance opportunities of empowerment, he promised entitlement. Maybe he persuaded the masses that it was their right to take from those who have worked hard to acquire a degree of wealth. This may have been his efforts toward Social Justice. The only problem with this theory is that when those of wealth are forced to distribute their resources to those whose belief system hinges on entitlements there will be no incentive for them continue their labors.

At what point, will the spirit of the *community* acquiesce to the ideology of entitlement? This paints a picture of a bland society where everyone lives with common precision, the only exception being those few special, elite people who represent the *institution*. They would be deemed worthy of a grandiose lifestyle. I believe even before Obama was sworn into office he began laying the groundwork for organizing an entitlement society.

This is a little story that gives the alternative to an entitlement society.

My father looked up when he heard the hissing and sputtering from a car that surrendered its last drop of fuel as it rolled to a stop in front of his barber shop. He could see four tiny expectant faces pressed against the smudged windows. The brow of the young woman seated in the passenger seat was creased with worry. The young driver opened the car door and stepped out with hesitancy. His steps were slow and cautious as he made his way toward the door of the shop. When he stepped inside his disheveled hair, frayed overalls, worn out shoes, and fearful eyes hinted of despair. My father asked if there was anything he could do for him.

The young man explained that he had four children and a wife in the car. He was a barber and asked if he could pick up some business in daddy's shop. He said he just needed enough barber business to buy a sack of bran or something to feed his family. The children were hungry and he had nothing to feed them. With haircuts ten cents and shaves fifteen, my father was scarcely making ends meet for our family.

It was very cold out. The man continued. He said if he could get some bran his wife could add water and make gruel for the children to eat. Since the car was their only home, they cooked in the dirt alongside the road. My father never doubted his desperation.

Alongside, attached to daddy's shop, was a vacant room. Daddy had rented the space for storing the bran we fed the cow kept in our backyard. The cow provided milk for our empty stomachs. What we didn't use, was bottled and sold door to door as we didn't have refrigeration to store it for later use. The milk supplemented our family resources.

Daddy told the family they were welcome to spend the night in the small room and to stay as long as it took to make other arrangements. Once inside from the cold, daddy gave the young man a full sack of bran. Then he went home and returned with a bottle of fresh milk.

The young man worked in daddy's barber shop until he had enough money to buy gasoline for their car. One morning, carrying with them the partial sack of bran, they climbed in the dilapidated Model A Ford and continued on their way.

My father's generous act was not an exception for the times. People helped one another. They didn't expect the government to step in with an entitlement program. People shared what they had. They had learned this lesson from their parents who had learned from their parents. It was a lesson passed from generation to generation. They did it because it was a moral, decent, life-saving thing to do. They did it because it was right.

We are charged to care and protect one another. Somehow in our self-centered, hurry-up world and with the erosion of the ethics that guide who we are in relation to our fellow man these values are diminishing.

As children we are born with compassion, love, faith, and respect toward human life. These are vetted in our souls. It is up to each of us to role model and nurture these innate qualities in our youngest citizens - our children.

In my opinion, attempts to legislate Social Justice do not work. It must be educated.

There seems to be an intentional effort to mask corruption in a cloak of fraudulent integrity and re-shape the psyche of the nation using the malicious tools of evil to crush good.

Keep in mind, Obama was born in the era of the Baby Boomers who were determined to disrupt the socio-economic status of America, if not the world, to forge an altered path that would set in motion policies that would change the nation forever. They believed it their right, if not their obligation, to use brutal force when attacking the principles held by the *community* of our great country. They took for granted the right to challenge the judiciousness of the *community*. Our nation needs to work toward unity. "Unity cannot be bought by force."

I cannot cite evidence of inspiration coming from the White House during these two years of Obama's presidency. His mode of operation appears to be ladened with mandates and edicts.

Of all the Presidents I have described, I have never feared the power of their influence over the *community*. Now I fear the preservation of democracy in our nation - fear the survival of our great nation.

Institution is a tool of the *community* designed to stand at the beckon call to support and respond to the needs of the *community* of people. Mutual respect, cooperation, honor, and unity should be the goal of the *institution* and of the *community*.

Through the years, the United States has suffered wars, pestilence, and the erosion of the self-worth of the nation. Most of the Presidents seem to have lived ethical and moral lives and have demonstrated high regard for the nation. Others have brought shame on the nation through their illicit behavior, dishonesty, and ill regard for the population. Their unethical behaviors have contributed to the decline in the morals of America. Our children look into the mirror at personalities in the highest office of the nation for evidence of what is right and what is real. In the seventy-five years of my lifetime, the deterioration of the high regard once claimed by the United States has been eroded away. Today, we live as a nation that has lost its sense of self and suffers the intimidation of shame and greed. Somehow we've got to find wise statesmen who can inspire the nation with visions of greatness. We must choose heroic leaders whose hearts plead for opportunities to preserve and defend the rights of all Americans. We must never align ourselves or fall prey to the bullies of the world. We must be vigilant in our search for politicians who carry out the governmental tasks of their office. Those politicians who operate in perpetual re-election campaign mode have lost their passion for representing the *community* they serve and need to step aside. We are desperate for politicians who "care" about the welfare of their constituents?

What sets the Presidents of past years apart from the current President? First of all, we the *community* went to the polling booths and cast ballots for the leaders of our nation. We must assume our responsibility for this dilemma. We intend our choices to be based on the candidate who cares the most about the welfare of the nation. In a free society, it is never certain how these things will come out. Sometimes the best person comes out on top and sometimes he/she doesn't. That is a reason we have congress to balance and equalize. With few exceptions, I believe previous Presidents in my lifetime have exuded a genuine desire to support the welfare of the nation. They may have committed personal indiscretions that lessened the status of America in the global world but somehow, in the midst of it all, they seem to have stayed focused on the needs of the *community*. On the other hand, the seated President, though no personal indiscretions seem to have escaped his closet, appears to operate with deceptions and distortions in the shaping of policies and legislation. I have seen no evidence of warm, genuine appreciation for the people of the nation. His orations ring cold and calculated unlike those of President Reagan when he said "Trust the People."

So, now what do we do? Continue on and I will offer my personal convictions for the restoration of America and for the growing of a kinder and gentler world.

Part Two

Growing
A
Moral Society

28.

There is a reason I paint this picture of the evolution of America and of the world of my lifetime. It is a selfish one. I hope these insights into the past will be of value as my family and others journey toward lives of integrity and passion.

I hope to be remembered as a person who lived with passion. The signature I attach to my e-mail messages reads, 'Let the passions of your soul fuel the dreams of your heart.' Truth is my most sought-after passion. I liken myself to the Sherlock Holmes of Scotland Yard in my search for truth. I am adamant in my quest to discover what is right and what is real. Truth, however rewarding or painful, is the moral compass that directs me toward claiming the goodness that is nestled in the heart of who I am. And, truth sets me free to chart a course that leads toward meaning and purpose. This gift comes from a power greater than I and is available to every living being.

I am an advocate of preserving childhood for every child born around the globe. You now know me to be one who is committed to unveiling deception in places that give it life. This points directly at the politics of the *institution*. More importantly, I hold an unshakeable faith in a loving God who sustains my courage to live a life of peace. To date, I have lived between the placidity of a largely rural nation and the global anger of the masses. My earlier writings have held clues to the role government plays in this evolution. Each administration has contributed either by omission or co-mission to the dilemma facing America.

29.

S ometimes the message slathered across our *community* and the world seems to be that we are losers expected to sacrifice our hard-earned resources, our self-worth, and our common decency toward mankind. I am not a great fan of football, but I think there is a reason the Oklahoma Sooner's football team is one of the best in the nation. Coach Bob Stoops doesn't use negative psychology to rally his players to greatness. He challenges and inspires them with positive visions of who they are and who they can become. WINNERS!! His mantra seems to be you are the best-you can win-go out there and be your best. Stoops hopes to empower his team to be the best and his team strives to make that a reality. I doubt if Bob Stoops aspires to be the President of the United States, but one thing is certain, he has discovered honor, respect, and a winning attitude are the ingredients that unite a team in its quest for greatness. I think there is a lesson to be learned here.

That lesson may be that mutual respect, cooperation, and honor are attitudes and beliefs that strengthen the bond between *institution* and *community*. Force is the demonic behavior of bullies.

For those who might share my suspicions on the probable dilemma facing our nation, I would like to offer some suggestions.

1. Try Love as a way to gain the respect of all nations. Be the role model of goodness, compassion, integrity, decency, ethics and morals.

2. Live in the faith that others are doing the best they can to live in decency towards others. Do not succumb to cynicism or indifference.

3. Identify your passions and do your little bit, whatever that may be, to make a difference in the world.

4.Be empowered to share your visions, convictions, and beliefs with others and resolve to do your part to make the world a better place.

5.When it comes to selecting leaders of the *institution* make sure you establish criteria contingent upon morals, integrity, and character regardless of race or political affiliation.

Whatever you choose to do let your voice be heard at the ballot box. Methodically observe, study, and scrutinize the words and behaviors of potential candidates. VOTE for ones who hold beliefs, values, and ethics that respect and honor the sacredness of the *community*. Look to those who probe their heart more than their head. Study behavior traits indicative of integrity and authenticity rather than deceitfulness and dishonesty; look for signs of detachment rather than engagement with the *community*. The study of body language reveals the soul of a person. There are books written on this. Do candidates inspire rather than denigrate? And do they exude goodness not malice? Do they understand unity as the by-product of mutual respect and not force? Do their actions lean more toward crushing the *community* than to affirming its greatness? These and more are characteristics to consider before you go into the ballot booth. Choose wisely and with intent. Morals, integrity, and decency are basic human traits indicative of worthy persons. They cannot be legislated. They are the foundation of a kinder, gentler society. In my way of thinking, they should be given priority in the education of our young.

30.

In these writings, I think it is clear the ethics that once brought admiration and honor to the *community* of the United States have eroded away. Recently, when interviewed by George Stephanopoulos on ABC's Good Morning America, Bill O'Reilly suggested that Obama has a problem with leadership. I believe his problem with leadership is born out of his decision to abandon the ethics of honesty and compassion to embrace dishonesty, coercion, deception, and manipulation. This compelling distinction between the roles of *institution* and *community* accurately depicts what is happening in America today. At a rapid pace, the *institution*, under the guardianship of Barack Obama, is sucking the life out of the *community* forcing it to run faster and faster to find balance and tranquility. Ethics and morals are at risk when expediency is the force that drives *institution* and engulfs *community*. The crisis that surrounds *institution* is self-imposed. The *community* crisis is the result of the threat of demise at the hands of the *institution*. Our moral compass is lost. Faith in the leadership of the *institution* to provide *community* support is lost.

Not long ago, a friend of mine expressed sadness for the divisiveness that is growing in our nation. She said if everyone would just leave things alone they would work out the way they are supposed to. I sometimes embrace that opinion. On the other hand, the world doesn't just leave things alone. It keeps on grinding forward, sometimes orderly, sometimes not so peacefully. My friend acquiesced in the circumstances that seem to divide us by saying, "It is in God's hands. I figure He will take care of it. Besides, there is nothing I can do. We just have to pray." I suggest to you, if our young men and women on the battlefield carried the same helpless attitude, we would have lost the freedoms we enjoy long ago.

I think the big question is, how do we heal ourselves of the guilt and shame written on the soul of America? How do we regain a new vision of who we are? How do we change the image reflected in our mirror? How do we restore the dignity and honor that was our identity. Is it possible for America to heal the wounds of slavery, wars, and ill-managed, inept actions?

So what can each of us do when ominous situations threaten to impose upon the morals and values we hold sacred?

1.   First, we can be kind.

2. We must delve into the soul of our nation and recapture the spirit of the *community*. From this we can begin the process of re-membering who we are. That is to say, we need to figure out how to pull together the fragmented pieces of ourselves and find the glue that binds us to a common goal of goodness. That glue is love, camaraderie, freedom, justice, and respect and it is found in the hearts of good men.

3. Prayer is a good place to begin. Prayers where God is allowed to put in His two-cents can reveal ways of understanding the situation. They can give new visions that point to the change that is needed. But prayer is not enough. God scatters bread crumbs. It is up to us to follow them.

4. Don't forget to pray for peace!

5. Communicate your concerns with others. Exchange ideas, views, and knowledge. Keep a dialogue going.

6. Sit down to rest and ponder where we are and how we are going to go forward.

7. Lay out a personal blueprint for making a difference. Your response may seem elemental, but if everyone made some contribution toward a solution, it would happen. It's those little bits of good put together that overwhelm the world.

8. And whatever you do, don't forget to be kind.

9. Spend time in contemplation and prayer as you wait for your soul to catch up.

10. And most of all, Love One Another. Love soothes and heals the wounds of guilt and sadness.

There is a greater power in charge of this planet and it is not us. God blesses us with inspired visions and asks us to be in charge of making them happen. Real change will happen as a result of the education of our young. In the writings that follow, I share a moment in time when I followed my passion for the education of young children. In 1972, I was privileged to share the birthing of Warm World an innovative early childhood school for young children and their families in Oklahoma City, Oklahoma. I hope my very existence is more than a bit of goodness in the world.

31.

The dilemma for man is that life can only be understood backwards; but it must be lived forward. The courage to move forward is rooted in the past. It is when you discover that the lifetime of your youth can no longer be taken for granted that you begin to reflect with compassion upon the blessings of your past and search for courage to write a new script for your future. Sometimes, people think looking back is the same as turning back. It suggests to them a return to living in the past. There are times we need to revisit the past to search through the rubble of our lives for the soul we left behind. Believing in the past is the springboard for believing in the present and the courage to believe in the hope of the future. I am convinced that goodness, integrity, wonder, joy, and hope are some of the original moral fibers in the soul of every individual. Life's circumstances have a way of disheveling the completeness of who we are. Through the act of looking back, we can begin the selective process of uniting (re-membering) the remnants of our original lives so that we might have the courage to move forward with a greater sense of who we are and who we hope to become. We are not people who turn back. We forge onward with great anticipation, heartfelt gratitude, and hopeful hearts toward the fulfillment of unimagined dreams.

The fall of 1970 was a dramatic turning point in my life. It was a time when the passions of my soul empowered the yearnings of my heart. I was a thirty-four-year-old housewife, a mother of a ten-year-old daughter, and an elementary school teacher. From my passion for the education of young children came a dream of developing a new and innovative early childhood school experience. I will discuss that later.

The moral education of our young is the fundamental purpose of education. It is the building of souls. I think William J. Bennett, former U.S. Secretary of Education, was right when he suggested the result of education should be thinking, feeling, concerned human beings who are skilled in pursuing personal fulfillment. There are some in the world of academia who would voice consternation toward those who assign it a secondary status while relational skills claim top billing. I believe it is better that we have people walking around who can't read or solve mathematical computations than it is for us to nurture into being a human society deficient in moral, ethical, and noble values. For those who hope to make a difference in the educational opportunities, it is imperative that they share a common belief that all parents love their children and want the best for them. Sometimes life's circumstances block their passion for making this the reality of their child. Children are to be nurtured in an environment that places a high priority on respect, acceptance, and appreciation for all of life--one that embraces the belief that all children are innately good, all children want to do their best, all children are in search of how they fit into the greater scheme of life.

Another time, William J. Bennett, offered a sincere and succinct understanding of why we should take the education of our young seriously. He indicated the desperate need to recover a sense of the fundamental purpose of education, which is to provide for the intellectual and moral education of the young. I believe we must re-invent our educational system. And the most critical issue that needs to be perpetually addressed is one that involves, specifically, the whole purpose of education. What should we hope to achieve in the education of our young? On occasion, an interesting scenario has been posed to parents. It goes like this. If you had a crystal ball or a magic wand, and could look into your child's future, what would you hope for him or her? In other words, what is the most significant gift you would give your child if it were in your power? Almost without hesitation, parents respond in a very simple way. I would hope that he would be a happy, well-adjusted person; that he would feel good about himself, that life would be fun and fulfilling for him, and that he would be inspired to discover his own unique way of making a difference in the lives of those around him. It is imperative, if not critical, that the educational society create a clear, specific definition of purpose. That means having a very direct and simple statement of philosophy - one that everyone can understand, interpret, and bring to life in the classroom.

It doesn't take a rocket scientist to know that the birth event of every human being is the impetus that shepherds in who they are and who they may become. I believe it is imperative that those charged with the creation of an educational experience for young children have a compassionate respect for the importance of the early years of life. The early years play a significant role in one's life and determine to a great extent, who he or she becomes as an adult. They are to be taken seriously. Education should be about preserving every child's right to a happy, secure childhood experience. Education should foster an awareness of the original goodness of every human being through the promotion of beliefs that all people are good. Our future rests in the hearts and souls of our children. I believe with these criteria in mind, we can find the keys to the creation of meaningful learning opportunities for our young. It is critical that children be given the tools to grow into strong, moral, and ethical individuals who hold sacred regard for human life. As far as I am concerned, education is about inspiring children to become the best human beings they can be. It is about encouraging children to dream beyond what they can see and create what they can imagine. Much of this happens in the home. Formal education points to, but is not limited to, literacy. As a society, we are charged with being a teacher to every other living being. Much of our teaching is through the role-modeling of our lives. Most of what happens in the environment of the society hinges on you and me and every one whose life touches that of a child. Whether intentionally or unintentionally, through our lives, we pass on the accepted principles of our society. Children deserve clear and specific messages regarding morals and ethics. We must not confuse them with a clouded sense of right and wrong, good and evil, sacred and obscene. It is our obligation to live with the just morals and ethical values that strengthen the significance of life - integrity, respect, compassion, and love.

I write about the education of our young children because I believe it and they are our only hope of restoring dignity and respect to the soul of our nation. I believe today, as I did in the seventies, that continuing the present paradigms regarding education will result in a faster and greater loss of the desired societal values, morals, and ethics. For too long, we have viewed the education of our young through the ill-defined lens of academia. I would like to suggest that this dilemma is of a societal nature, one not limited to the home or the educational system, but strangled by policy, dictated by routine, and steeped with the ordinary rather than with the exceptional. I join with many others in attempts to analyze the shortcomings of the present educational climate. Everyone lays claim to specific concerns. My passion for children and life compels me to question why the decline in academic achievement, why the school drop-out rate is so high and why so many juveniles are in trouble.

I believe we must keep questioning until we find some definitive answers. A multitude of new approaches to teaching have been tried; investment in the latest technology; infuse the system with money. Yet, none of these have made a dramatic difference. Our children are still struggling. It is obvious that what we are doing is not working. So what is the key to this crisis?

I confess that the assumptions and generalizations I make come from my thirty-two years of experience working with children and families. Many times these two entities (children and parents) are credited with blocking the literacy of our young. But I believe this condition denotes the inclusive and invasive nature of our society, namely, the lack of regard and respect for the sacredness surrounding the lives of our young. It seems that for every family in awe of the life of their child, many others take for granted their very presence, and for some a child is a nuisance to be endured.

Emiley and I have a special friendship. She is twenty-months old. I have known her since her birth. Every Sunday, when Emiley and her parents arrive for worship, her little eyes search the congregation in hopes of finding a familiar face. I am always happy when she recognizes me and runs to show me her 'blankey' or her sparkly red 'Dorothy' shoes. Emiley's parents believe she is a gift to be treasured, to be nurtured, and to be loved. She is blessed with parents who honor who she is as a human being. They are her role models. They are her cheerleaders. They delight in her successes. They believe it is their privilege to parent Emiley in her process of growing into who she is to become as a responsible, caring adult. I've heard it said that every child needs at least one person who revels in their very existence - someone who believes in them. Emiley is one lucky little person. She lives with an innate sense that she is valued for who she is, that she is worthy of respect. Her soul is intact. There are many others out there who, unlike Emiley, don't experience what it is to have two parents who believe they are a precious gift, who delight in their every discovery, and who guard and protect them from the ravages of the world. I believe that as long as children are delegated to a lesser status in the world, all the educational tools, all the latest technology, cannot heal the voids in their lives nor guide them into a bright future. As parents and educators, all we can do is grieve the loss when the innate sparkle has gone out of their young lives. We can only give support as they struggle to cope in a demanding world. Once neglected, the wonders and mysteries of childhood can never be recaptured. What impact does that make on the quality of life for a child? How do we inspire parents to rise above the disparities of their young experiences to love their offspring?

Hildegard Bingen (a medieval visionary who lived between 1098 and1179) once said, "There is no higher state in life than childhood." If that is so, and I believe it is, why don't we give special attention to honoring the young years of a child's life? You may not believe this, but there was and remains to be those who look in the cradle and see a helpless bundle of something. They are not sure just what it is. Many do not recognize the personhood of a child. Children are little people who grow up to be adult people. It is imperative that each of us assumes responsibility for nurturing the unfolding of their lives. Savor their early years. Fill your memory bank with the many wonders of who they are. The wealth of your memory chest will provide the strength and courage you will need to help them as they begin to chart their journey through life.

I would suggest that education should be a simple process. Instead it has been made into a worrisome and complex system wrought with failure. We have joined the competitive Baby Boomer race plaguing our nation since the sixties. It is a race to change the world, and to change it fast. Some earlier generations were so driven in their quest to change the world they were willing to forfeit childhood to get on with becoming self-sustaining, independent, productive individuals. They didn't consider the ramifications of denying a child the opportunity to progress through the predictable stages of childhood. They had no idea the damage inflicted on the child who is rushed through each stage of his life with little time to explore, discover, and bask in just being a child. Further, they didn't take into account the damage done to an entire nation. Many times, depriving children of their rightful gift of a childhood filled with rich and innovative experiences results in children who are dependent, despondent, discouraged, and perhaps even illiterate. Children robbed of their childhood may have difficulty with issues involving morals, ethics, trust and faith in a supreme being.

The crucial component of the classroom is the teacher. Everything hinges on his or her desire to make a difference in the lives of children. Wherever that attitude is present you will find energetic, creative, innovative teachers. School districts can invest in all kinds of materials, the latest technology, and beautiful classrooms, but if the teacher is not suited for the job, children and learning will be at risk. School administrators must have a clear understanding of the significance of the developmental characteristics of young children. They must have a keen sense of the eloquent characteristics of teachers who come forth to carry the heart of each child within them.

Make no doubt about it, I believe children are the purest exemplifications of goodness in the world. As a person of faith, I believe children arrive fresh, vibrant, and with an eternal spirit that offers renewed hope in the midst of our weary world.

Several years ago, a minister friend relayed this touching story to me. It seems a young couple in his congregation had been blessed with the arrival of their second child, Rachel. Peter, their three-year-old, also known as THE big brother, had looked forward to this event with great anticipation. He could hardly wait for Mom and Dad to bring his new sister home. The young parents had been preparing Peter for this special day. They were taken back a bit as Peter began requesting time alone with the new baby. They felt certain it would be safe yet, they couldn't help wondering why he was so insistent. And after giving it some thought they agreed to grant his request. As his parent's waited outside the partially open door, Peter tiptoed into Rachel's room. He stood beside the crib, his tender gaze searching her sleepy face. Very gently he grasped her tiny fingers and began to speak in a near whisper to his new sibling, "Tell me what He looked like," Peter queried. "It has been so long since I've seen Him I've almost forgotten how He looked." He continued to look at Rachel as he delicately stroked her head, and after waiting a few moments for her to awaken with a response to his serious inquiry he turned and tiptoed out of the nursery.

How can it be that in such a short while after our transformation into the human realm of existence we too, like Peter, lose sight of the spiritual bonds of our original birth? Could it be that the lengthening of our basic umbilical cord creates a sense of unrest within each of us? In turn, perhaps that innate unrest becomes the catalyst propelling each of us into a perpetual life journey – a journey focused on strengthening the linkage of the world of our beginning with the world of our present. Perhaps, at a very deep level, we are like Stephen Spielberg's movie character E.T. We feel the gentle tug and hear the quiet voice continually reminding us that we belong to a greater source in another realm. We fear getting too far away from home lest we forget who we are and whose we are.

How do we awaken the innate yearnings within the hearts of parents, teachers, grocers, ministers, and all other people to be a gentle, mindful presence in the midst of these tender lives? This is a sacred childhood issue because it is where adulthood has its roots. If the roots are nurtured in childhood, there is a greater chance that adulthood will be a joy-filled, rewarding life experience. Children who are affirmed for who they are and inspired to become all they can be have a greater propensity to lead happy, successful lives.

So what does this say about children and childhood? It says a mystery surrounds the life of each newborn. It points to the significance of protecting and preserving the sacredness of that mystery. What does it say about the educating of our young? First of all, it says that parents are the most important teachers a child will ever have. They hold the keys to the moral and ethical behavior a child absorbs. The acts and stimulus in every moment of life are learning moments for a child, or for any of us for that matter. Prescribed and structured learning environments must foster a keen sense of appreciation regarding the specialness of every child. That specialness is the beacon that lights the way for our young to learn how they fit into the scheme of life in an awesome world. Secondly, there must be an alliance with home and school. Education cannot be a matter of compartmentalizing - parents or teachers. It is an integrative process involving parents, teachers, and anyone else whose life touches that of a child's.

In my early years, the first eight grades of learning happened in a one-room country school where parents and educators worked together to insure the educational progress of the child and of the school. Teachers were respected for their devotion to the responsibility of teaching children the necessary skills to cope and live in the world. A positive line of communication was established between parents and teachers. Parents believed in their child's ability to learn the required materials and were proud to be the first teacher and personal advocate. Parents monitored their child through the demands of homework. They read to their children. They were supportive of the teacher and of the school. If little 'Johnny' had difficulty at school, parents were the first responders. They assumed it was their duty as parents to discover the source of the issue. Parents collaborated with the teacher to design a plan that would alleviate the concern. It was a plan to encourage the child to assume responsibility for learning and for his behavioral attitudes.

Each of us is innately hard-wired with desires to nurture and care for our young. For some, for whatever reason, there is a short-circuit in that connection. Young adults entertaining the prospect of having children would do well to examine their desires to become parents. Should they discover that parenting another's life is out of the range of their imagination, I would suggest they use a little more time before assuming the role. Children deserve to be received into a loving family - one that delights in who they are, one that is in awe of their every new discovery. Most parents love their children and want the best for them. I believe their greatest hope for a child is that he or she become a happy, productive, emotionally secure person who is capable of coping and living in our changing world. Most parents place a lessor priority on their child becoming a rocket scientist or even the President of the United States.

It is my belief that with World War II and the temporary absence of one or both parents, with mothers joining the work force outside the home, with the explosion of the technological age, with the cataclysmic effects of the *Summer of Love* and the detachment from the anchor of parental protection, the nuclear family has all but disintegrated. Parents struggle to keep pace as the societal structures force them onward. It seems, before parents can adapt to one stage of parenting, they are pummeled into the next one. There is no time or energy to Be with their child; to read with them; to review homework; to bask in the joy and delight of their child's accomplishments. I think, at times, parents feel helpless and alone - exhausted and depressed - making it easier to abdicate the role as their child's most important teacher to the educational system. Today teachers are expected to assume the responsibility for teaching academic concepts, social skills, emotional well-being and behavioral attitudes. Children are confused and lost in the cracks between home and school. With so many, yet so few, adults looking out for the welfare of our children, children are at risk of becoming fearful, insecure, and unhappy. I believe this is definitive of a nation running without a soul. We must make an orchestrated effort to form an alliance with schools and families. To do otherwise, facilitates the continual downward spiral of the ethics, the morals, and the intellect of our culture.

Fifteen years into my career of teaching first through sixth grade children, I was wrought with concern over the disregard surrounding the sacredness of childhood. The range of my classroom experience was kindergarten through sixth grade with the greater part being spent in first grade. I discovered, as the escalating demands of society closed in around young parents, they were coerced into sacrificing their child's early years for the expectations of a later time. Children were placed in child care outside the home. In an effort for parents to compensate for the lack of time spent with their children, they enrolled them in every stimulating program available - T-ball, soccer, piano lessons, ballet, and the list goes on. Not wanting to neglect their child's cognitive skills nor risk their child being behind those of his/her peers, parents sought early learning programs. Many of those programs surrendered the sacredness of childhood to concentrate on skills belonging to a later age. From birth on, children should be given quiet, uncommitted time to ponder and to wonder about their surroundings and their existence. Instead, they have fallen prey to a nation consumed with a 'sooner and faster' ideology. Young children are being pushed academically at the expense of developing crucial social and problem solving skills. The expertise of educational *institutions* promotes literacy in areas of language arts, math, science, and social studies. But, these constitute only a portion of what a child needs to live in a civilized society. I believe it is critical for children to be involved in programs rich with social, emotional, and behavioral learnings - without which, they are crippled for life. When educational *institutions* are asked to create programs for three and four-year-olds, they tend to use the same academic model as those for older children. The result being that young children are subjected to learning environments where the 'process' is sacrificed for an end 'product.' Programs of structure take priority over experiential learning. Academic expectations of Kindergarten are pushed down to preschool robbing children of their precious early years of childhood. In order for children to do well in school they must be able to cope and learn at the same time.

I am convinced a warm and safe childhood, free from the burdens of adult responsibilities, is the right of every child. There are those who would argue that children of today are exposed to so much technology that they are more advanced in their learning compared with children of the fifties or sixties. Various human development studies have attempted to document infant and child growth and development. Their primary hope is that all children have the privilege of enjoying childhood and have the time and opportunity to grow and to learn at their own pace and in their own way. Such studies point out children are developing at the same rate neurologically as they did in earlier years, still they are being pushed to do everything sooner. For a short time, children muster the courage and sustaining power to cope with hurried expectations. At some point, they become discouraged and shut down their interest to learn. These studies further theorize that children who learn to read by age four have no advantage by third grade over children who master reading at five or six years old. So what is the point of speeding up a child's academic performance? Why sacrifice their early years for the needs and the expectations of a later time? First, for some, it is to elevate the altered egos of young parents. Secondly, I suggest to you, that some parents become anxious when they take note of the bright and resilient little person living with them. They fear the loss of that brilliance if not tapped immediately. Disregarding a damaging event in a child's life, intelligence will not go away. It is theirs for a lifetime. In the sequential order of time and surrounded by a rich and nurturing environment the intellect will expand. The years of a child's life defined with early education are essential in providing proper experiences and exploration rather than learning their letters earlier. When young children are put on a fast track to learning academic concepts their childhood is at risk of being compromised. No doubt, children of yesterday and today are bright little beings. Regardless of their exposures, they remain children who deserve to have the luxury of being a child for at least the first five years. Those are the years when every child should be afforded rich, stimulating, awe-inspiring experiences that encourage success in the discovery of joy surrounding childhood. With these understandings and convictions, I was wrought with concern over the plight of young children. I questioned then, and again today, the right of parents, educators, and society to rob children of their childhood.

In 1970, I was teaching first grade when this dilemma became more apparent. The class groupings were assembled according to ability. Students were ranked by the level of their performance. Keep in mind, these were six-year-olds. They had one year of kindergarten under their belts and were already being labeled above average, average, and SLOW. I know the rationale that teachers can be more effective when classrooms are clustered around students of like abilities. There is validity to that. Arguments can be made on many sides of that issue. For me, a product of a one-room country school with children in grades one through eight, I know the advantages of learning in an environment with students of various levels of learning. The easy, less structured setting and the repetition of material introduced to those in other grade levels reinforces and inspires children to learn beyond their appointed curriculum.

The year I was assigned the so-called SLOW learners was a great year for me and the children. It was the year when my passion for children laid its claim on me. I was completing my Master of Arts in Teaching degree. The thesis of my final paper outlined the correlation between teaching language arts and creative dramatics. What I learned about those students was that instead of being SLOW learners they were children who were over-placed in school. They were bright children who were chronologically old enough to be in first grade, but they were developmentally young. This resulted in them not being ready to assume and master the tasks expected in the classroom. Instead of SLOW learners, they were young learners. Some had delayed small motor-skills, others were still learning how to follow directions or to play cooperatively in the sandbox. For some, counting to ten and writing their name was a challenge.

Every morning as the sun was beginning to come up over the horizon, Susan was rousted out of bed, dressed and taken to daycare. She had her 6th birthday on August 15, making her eligible for first grade. She was a short and delightfully round little girl with deep brown eyes and a gentle smile. Both of her parents worked outside the home. When she arrived at the day care she was given a nutritious breakfast and time to play for an hour or so. Precisely at 8:45 a.m. Susan climbed aboard a van loaded with several other children and made the short trip to school. I remember Susan very well. She was a student in my first grade class. Her entrance to the classroom was cautious. After finding her desk, she would nestle into her space and begin organizing her spelling book, her reader, her numbers workbook, and her pencils. Now she was ready to begin the day.

Susan labored over the tasks that most first graders whizzed through. She knew what to do but it just took her a little longer. Soon after the school day began, Susan began to wriggle around. Either the desk was too high or her legs were too short. In any case, her feet began to dangled forwards and backwards. It was plain to see, she was uncomfortable at her desk and uncomfortable with the required tasks.

When it came time for creative dramatics and music and art, Susan came alive. The filmy scarf she twirled above her head as she danced to Up, Up And Away In My Beautiful Balloon gave the appearance of a lovely little ballerina. Susan felt happy when she danced. It was fun. It was pretend and Susan could be anyone she wanted to be. The teacher talked about words and numbers and colors. What Susan didn't know was that she was learning to read and count in a different way. She had found something she could do and it was good.

As it turned out, Susan was a bright child who was developmentally young. When given an extra year to grow into herself, she could focus on the challenges of first grade. I discovered others in her same circumstance - bright children who were not ready to cope with the distractions of the classroom and not ready to learn the required tasks. Many children fall into this circumstance. When recognized, a special curriculum can be designed to fit where they are socially, emotionally, behaviorally, and intellectually. This can help to take the stress off children and give opportunities for success in learning. Success makes children happy. Happy children learn better and feel good about themselves.

There is a tool that measures a child's readiness for school. It provides parents and teachers information about their child's developmental age. One tool designed for the discovery of this data was created by the Gesell Institute in New Haven, Connecticut. It is administered and scored by skilled educators. It can be very helpful and reassuring to parents. I advise parents to look into this assessment.

My classroom became a different kind of learning lab before learning labs were popular. Reading and math skills were presented through creative music, art, and drama. Even though the Principal raised an eyebrow when he entered the classroom to discover all of us dancing with magic scarves, I was convinced these were bright children. I believe children learn through experiences of success. In the creative arts, any sincere expression is acceptable and considered a success. Children grow in self-confidence when they are affirmed for who they are and not for just how they perform academically.

Some of these children advanced to second grade. Most were given the privilege of visiting first grade another year. More importantly, most had a fun time and enjoyed successes that build confidence and self worth.

As with so many things in life, we try to speed children up, forcing them into expectations belonging to another time and stealing their rightful time to be a child. The bottom-line is that parents and teachers should not treat all children as ready for the same thing at the same time.

In June of 1992, the front page headlines in the Daily Oklahoman read: TEEN FINISHES COLLEGE, RETURNS TO HIGH SCHOOL. (Copyright 1992, The

Oklahoman Publishing Company) This is a story of a very bright young man, one who was wise enough to know that if he surrendered his youth to adult expectations he would never have another opportunity to experience the activities and relationships of his peers.

The story focused on a young man who, at age thirteen, became the youngest student ever to attend the University of Oklahoma. He graduated from the university at sixteen and was accepted in the college of medicine. To the surprise of many, he declined the offer to enter medical school. Instead, he requested an opportunity to return to his former high school to complete his senior year with his previous classmates. He said, "I've been away from my friends and social activities for four years. I'd like to see some of my friends who I've known since the first grade." He went on to say he wanted to attend the prom, to play basketball, and to be in the high school yearbook.

His father said, "He missed talking and interacting with friends of the same age."

The author of the story, Jim Killackey, concluded by saying, "It appears the young man wants to make sure the experiences of youth don't elude him forever."

This story supports an idea embraced by early childhood specialists: life offers us the opportunity to progress through predictable stages. There is a specific time in our life-span to experience what it is like to be a child and participate in child-like activities. If we by-pass a stage of our childhood, there will always be a void in that place of our development. More than likely, sometime in our life we may make futile attempts to recapture those precious lost moments. To behave like a four-year-old or fifteen-year-old at thirty-five is inappropriate. I believe the message of this story is that of a young man trying to protect his soul.

In Rachel Carson's book The Sense of Wonder, she notes the profound and innate yearnings of childhood. Far too often those awe-inspiring wonders are dampened or even lost in our early years. If each of us was granted the right to give our children a gift of hope in all that surrounds them, we would want them to know joy and delight and quiet inner peace.

32.

In 1970, my concerns for the education of young children began taking shape. I traded my classroom in public school for one in a private school setting with twenty, three-year-olds and on alternating days twenty, four-year-olds. I was convinced then and remain so today, that the only way we can expect to restore and preserve the goodness and integrity of our society is through the education of our children. To me, the values and perceptions they hold are the foundations that support a compassionate *community*. The world needs more people who live with good morals and values. They are the ones who make the world stronger. They make competent decisions of integrity.

Much of the time we believe the trickle-down theory applies to educating our young. I believe in laying a foundation and building up. Some schools begin offering fine arts activities - music, art, library privileges - in second grade. It is believed kindergarten and first grade children have not mastered the necessary skills to justify access to these activities. I believe in the creation of an educational atmosphere that supports children as they build a foundation of learning to live in the world. It was and is my opinion that when children grow in respect for themselves and for all of creation then, and only then, will we know a softer, gentler world. Everyone can do their 'little bit' to make a difference in the world we bequeath to our children.

On a wall of my church, there was a banner with this inspiring message: "And God saw all that he had created and it was good." Every child is a unique creation of God. They are here on a specific mission, as equally appointed as those big persons who receive them. Then, why is it we don't nurture an awareness of their innate goodness, and value the gifts they bring? Why do we feel compelled to hurriedly strip off their "swaddling clothes" and anxiously speed them on toward the future stages of their lives?

In the grip of this powerful passion to hopefully find a way to make a difference in societal appreciation of the early years in a child's life, it was not enough to merely be heard by a sympathetic ear. There was the desire to find specific ways of impacting the existing condition levied at children.

Still, how does one go about recreating the mystic sense of wonder and reverence surrounding the life of every young child after it has been pushed aside to make way for other priorities? Is it possible to completely regenerate a person's spiritual self when it has been left dormant for a period of years? How do we kindle the fire of life? Do the original wrappings enfold the same person when rebound later in life, or is there an empty chasm at the very depth of our being?

My anguish over these concerns was shared by my friend and his wife, who incidentally had been an elementary teacher as well.

Near the end of our discussion, a poignant question was raised. "How do you think this situation could be changed?"

I wasn't sure how to answer. Still after a few seconds, I said, "I guess a person could start a school of their own."

"Well, why don't you do that?" my friend asked.

Twenty some years later, and my memory a little dim, I suspect I responded with a little, unsure laugh. I had no idea the conversation would evolve to this point. He was challenging me to step through a door that could lead to making a meaningful difference in the lives of young children--an opportunity to craft an environment which would encourage, enhance, and enlighten their sense of becoming who they are created to be. It was my chance to explore significant options for impacting the experiences of their early years. The choice could be mine. I could get down in the trenches, and work toward creating fresh, new visions of what an exciting, joyful childhood might look like. Or I could passively ride the prevailing tide of indifference regarding the plight of young children.

Once again, my friend posed the question. "Why don't you start a school, one that would be an alternative for parents who want a richer, more fulfilling childhood experience for their young children?"

Whoa! Me start a school? I had never seriously entertained such an idea. Besides, I was teaching in public school. I didn't know anything about little people younger than kindergarten age. Then again, the more I thought about it I realized I did know something. I knew a lot about young children.

Often I have been told I am idealistic. I take that as a compliment. Coupled with the nature of a risk-taker, I am free to dream possibilities beyond what I could ever imagine.

Even before my friend said good-by, I was beginning an uncharted journey into the dreams of new childhood frontiers, exciting and filled with wonder.

A small group of others, who shared my concerns as well as my dreams for children decided to pool their thoughts. They trusted the strength of their combined efforts to facilitate the dreaming of new dreams. And their visions evolved around the significance of the early years of a child's life. The consensus of the group was that these were the years that would determine to a great extent who a child would become as an adult.

As the group indulged in their fantasies of what the early years in a child's structured learning experiences might include, the dream began to creatively assume a specific form. The result of these efforts was the conception and birth of a unique school called Warm World.

It was my privilege to have shared in this initial dream. More importantly, I was honored to have become the founder and director of this beautiful expression of affirmation regarding the young lives of children.

As I reflect on this event in my life, I feel much like Moses might have felt when he heard God speaking to him through a burning bush.

Who, Lord? Are you talking to me? What's that you say? You want me to start a school for young children? But, Lord, I'm just a teacher. Ask Mary Jones. She's the lady you want for this job. No. You want me to do it? But, Lord, how will I know what to do? What's that you say, Lord? You will show me how?

With the help and support of many of God's disciples, the seeds for a warm and wonderful world are being generously strewn. I am eternally grateful I heard His voice in the cries of the children and said, "Yes" to receiving the gift that would enable me to become personally involved in making a difference in the lives of young children.

Children - people who are loved and valued, tend to feel good about themselves and lead happy meaningful lives.

What sets Warm World apart from other early childhood schools?

The primary factor that distinguishes Warm World from many other schools for young children is a clear and succinct philosophy whose distinctive characteristic is one that honors all human life. It places emphasis on preserving childhood, nurturing creativity, developing social skills, and building self-confidence. It is believed that the early years of a child's life are crucial for developing foundations of self-worth without which all other achievements become difficult, if not meaningless.

It is believed that the early years determine, to a great extent, who a child becomes in adult life. Much attention is given to creative experiences that are success driven and stimulate a child's sense of wonder. It is believed that creative music, creative drama, and creative art provide the foundation for all learning, especially the learning of intellectual and cognitive skills. It is critical to have an outstanding staff who embraces the philosophy and whose primary concern is creating unique and innovative activities and experiences that nurture a child's soul. A small pupil/teacher ratio allows for a personal relationship with every child - a relationship where every child enjoys the privilege of one teacher who is compassionately interested in their ideas, their accomplishments, and their needs. The physical atmosphere is steeped with bright colors that suggest freedom to explore and learn through discovery. Equipment and materials are selected for their experiential and concrete learning - ones that spark a child's curiosity to learn.

The wonder and magic of Warm World continues today. In the nineteen years I served as the founder/director, I was blessed by a host of intentional parents who chose Warm World as an exciting and nurturing learning environment for their children. I am forever grateful for the trust and confidence they placed in me and in the school.

A warm, happy, safe childhood filled with rich, wonder-filled experiences is the right of every child. Furthermore, I am convinced that the beliefs held by those who birthed Warm World are relevant for all children including those in high school and especially those in alternative educational experiences. It is up to us to figure out how we can make that happen. I suggest that our present educational system is somewhat like the *institution* and our children are like the *community*. When the smooth operations of the system take precedence over the well-being of the children, children are at risk of being forced to drop their souls and leave them behind.

I have had the privilege to follow many of the children who participated in this unique and innovative Warm World experience. To share the magic of their beautiful childhood years, was a divine gift. Today, some are accomplished lawyers, doctors, artists, musicians and others have followed dreams into exciting endeavors. One works in the Pentagon on secret projects involving the security of our nation. More important, most are happy, emotionally secure people who cope and live in the sometimes distraught world. My heart has been deeply touched by their lives. They bear hope in the soul of man. I applaud the fervent quest of brave parents who risked stepping outside the box of an ordinary learning experience so their child could participate in the extraordinary. I am honored they chose Warm World.

Blessed be childhood, as children are the purest exemplifications of the goodness of life. It is the responsibility of every adult to honor the sacredness of children. I believe the only way to re-ignite morals and ethics in our nation is through the education of our children.

Today, cries of disappointment and blame surround the dilemma of the educational system in our nation. Society expresses frustration over its broken and ineffective educational system. Government promises an overhaul of requirements and regulations. States want more money. Unions strong-arm congress over matters involving tenure and control of *institutional* policies. Classroom teachers ask for lower pupil/teacher ratios, money for supplies, and increased salaries. And the dance goes on. All entities make valid requests. We've tried throwing more money into the coffers of educational *institutions*. We've equipped most schools with the latest technology. Still test scores suffer. So how do we get a handle on the situation? I would like to suggest the implementation of a new philosophy, much like the one at Warm World. Pull together intelligent, compassionate, energetic, creative persons made vulnerable by their passions for young children and inspire them to dream outside the box of academia. Charge them with creating a philosophy of education that is simple and easy. Require them to answer questions like: Why do we educate our young? If you had the power to give children anything in the world, what would it be? I hope the answers to these two questions would be something like educating happy, emotionally secure, responsibly productive individuals for a meaningful life experience. Make morals and ethics a priority. The well-being of our children, families, and our nation is at stake. We must begin now.

In our nation are brilliant young minds whose innate intellect inspires their desire to grow, expand, experiment, explore, and discover the perimeters of the unknown. Theirs is a gift that will not be denied. In a nurturing environment, where success is the goal, all children achieve at a higher rate. I didn't say all children will be doctors or lawyers or executives. I said all children learn at a higher rate of proficiency when success is the goal. Varying degrees of success are achievable. Success makes people happy. Happiness is good. Yes, I believe in literacy. It is critical that every capable child learn to read and to do basic math computations. We must discover what it means to integrate literacy and morals and ethics into education. Together they offer a sense of balance that allows each of us to live less stressful and more meaningful lives.

I need it said that I have concerns about the mix of young children, mechanical technology, and education. A few days ago, I heard someone lamenting the possibility of cursive writing being taken out of the curriculum. I think the assumption is that the written communication preferences of young children have evolved to a form of printing letter/word symbols and/or are computer driven. The lamenting thought expressed is of a neurological nature and one I think holds validity. It is in the process of repetitive practicing of writing skills the brain imprints valuable symbols that enhance cognitive learning. When my first grade teacher, Sadie Lawton, assigned Mrs. Kettles Penmanship Exercises to the forty children in my one-room country school, she hoped for legibility. She didn't have a clue that what she was teaching influenced more than writing skills. The discipline of intense focusing on this task spilled over into all of learning. I hasten to say that I don't think the teaching of writing in schools has been abandoned. It has been incorporated into other areas of the curriculum.

As technology (computers, I-Phones, I-Pads, and such) continues to take command of everything we do, I become concerned about their long-range implications for children and future generations. I love my computer and I delight in the adeptness of young children to surf around the internet. They are free of the intimidations that tend to paralyze adults. New technology and programs are amazing. Although computers never seem to make the significant difference hoped for in the learning that needs to happen in the classroom. I'm not sure that the use of computers have made a difference in achievement scores. For whatever reason, the razzle-dazzle of the gadgetry has its limitations. There is no replacement for the gentle guidance of a teacher who cares. It seems obvious to me that we need to examine the advantages and disadvantages of financial resources invested in mechanical technology used to motivate children to learn.

On behalf of our culture, there is the tendency to become so immersed in the great potential of the new and innovative ideas and techniques that we fail to look for possible hazards. We go overboard and use computers for the 'one size fits all' approach. Could it be that computer-driven teaching methods in the primary grades gets in the way of cognitive learning? By that I mean, is it possible that a child's retrievable learning is more on the manipulation of the computer and less on the concepts? No doubt, children are learning in their mastery of technology. They are little geniuses in their search across the waves of the internet. What if computer learning doesn't imprint on the brain in the same way our physical senses do? What if the intense focus of children on the gimmickry of the computer is leaving the retention of concepts wandering somewhere in the recesses of the brain? I wonder if teachers are being asked to sacrifice their personal effectiveness in teaching the basic skills and concepts. Do they expend precious energy focusing on the mastery of the latest mechanical teaching tools that may or may not impede their ability to attend to the particular needs of each child in their classroom? Most teachers are dedicated, intentional, caring people. They exhaust every possible resource to maximize each child's learning potential.

I don't have the answers to these questions. But it is clear something is missing from our formula to create a promising and credible educational system in the United States. Go to Braums or Wal Mart. Many of the young checkers cannot make change without the help of the computer. If the computer fails, they are lost. It is critical that everyone in society, who is of able mind, have at their command the basic skills of math, language, rational thinking, common sense, and relational civility. Earlier, I termed us as a 'throw away' society. I am concerned we might become a 'throw away' society of mind-held knowledge. It is good to be empowered with knowledge that is imprinted on the brain. If we continue our dependency on computer technology, how long will it be before our culture is a brainless society? At some point, there is the risk that technology will take over the functions of the brain and consume thought. What happens to social relational skills with extended engagement with computers and such? It is not difficult to imagine a time when educational advocates will demand that computers be given the status of extra-curricular and the imprinting of cognitive skills returned to the priority.

Like so many of our indulgences, when we become enamored with the gadgetry, we go overboard and let the use of it consume our better sense. At what point will we know the pendulum has swung too far and the potential harm outweighs the benefits? Then how will we right the system? Computers have their place in the educational arena. We need both technology and thinking minds in our society. A world without thinking minds will be void of creative technology.

Time is of the essence. The well-being of our children is at stake. We can no longer require schools and teachers to be the sole carriers of the burden of teaching everything to our children. As responsible parenting of our young abdicates its role, teachers are the ones who are in the trenches mining the depths of a child's potential with every tool possible. It is every person's responsibility to claim their role as teacher to our young; parents, educators, the waitress at McDonalds, the mailman, and more important, the politicians who are in charge of the *institution* of America. That means the President - especially the President. The role model they provide should be without blemish. I am ashamed of the current President's decisions to surround himself with persons who, in my opinion, have less than honorable backgrounds. To date, the corruption of deceit and dishonesty, of unpaid taxes, support of radical groups, self-interest involvements, and coercion place a cloud of evil over the *institution*. How can we expect morals and ethics from our youth when they are bombarded with despicable adult behavior? How can we expect them to behave with respect and kindness toward others when our politicians feel entitled to do, or say, whatever might be advantageous in their pursuit of office? What does it say to our young when news anchors spew twisted truths to persuade toward a particular point of view?

Our lives must be examples of compassion and truth. We are all teachers. It takes all of us working together to create and support an environment that encourages the reputable moral and ethical behavior of our young.

When Steffan, my nephew, was fourteen-years-old, his father, Marion died unexpectedly of a massive heart attack. Steffan and his father had been great friends. Marion was always there for Steffan. He took him to school every day and attended all his basketball games and could be found center-court in the bleachers. He basked in the blessing of Steffan's life. Marion was a parent who played an active role in the life and education of his child. He read with him, had meaningful conversations with him, created with him, dreamed with him, he imagined with him. As Steffan and his mother gathered at the kitchen table to begin the process of gathering up the pieces of their lives he said, "But, Mother, who will inspire me now?" His mother assured him that she would be there to inspire him and attend to his needs. All of us need someone to support and nurture and care for us as we navigate the waters of life - someone who believes in us - someone who loves us - someone who inspires us to become all we can be.

To solve this crucial dilemma happening to our children and to the future of our society, we must glean from past successes in the classroom and use those as the foundation for creating new paradigms toward raising educational standards for all. There are three reasons I share my passions for education. First, I believe the levity through which we educate our young determines the strength of the foundation upon which we create a moral, ethical, and literate society. Second, I am an educator. You are an educator. It is up to each of us to be about finding the keys to a kinder, gentler world. Third, and most important, all of us must join in the quest to stop the race that leads to nowhere when we run without a soul. I will admit my assumptions regarding the dilemma of education may be somewhat idealistic. My solutions may sound simple but I know without a doubt that the Warm World experience is one that works. I believe we must scratch our heads, rack our brains, ask all the questions we can in our quest to create an educational system that supports more than literacy. It must be one that equips our young with the tools to enjoy a rich and meaningful life.

The way I see it, the ineffectiveness of our educational system plays a significant role in the continuum of our troubled society. Considering suicide is the third leading cause of death in young persons between the ages of 15 and 24, we have two choices: we can pay for the re-visioning of a clear and succinct philosophy of education that will nurture, encourage, and empower our young as they grow into mature, responsible, compassionate, contributing individuals; or we can invest in more places of therapeutic rehabilitation for our young, discouraged adolescents. For some, this may include incarceration facilities.

As I conclude my thoughts on education, I am remembering that during the Presidency of Franklin Delano Roosevelt in the forties, the United States had a policy of neutrality - of staying the course - of not becoming involved in disputes in other countries - of honoring the soul of America. Perhaps we should revive that policy. Today, under the trickling-down influence of the power-driven generations, our nation appears to run with abandon. Maybe it is easier to think of patching the wounds of the nation than it is to dream and strategize how to grow a nation toward wellness. Perhaps it runs because the innate call of the soul is to goodness - goodness is dependent upon the staying power of truth, honesty, decency, and compassion.

I suspect fear and urgency regarding the condition of the educational situation propels the nation toward a 'quick fix'. Methodical, well thought strategizing, and precious time are the keys to the evolution of a literate, compassionate, and moral society. Perhaps, it is easier to run than it is to wait for the eyes of the soul to pierce the darkness of our lives and light our way toward an authentic life of honor. And so we run.

33.

At the risk of sounding redundant, I want to be specific in the purpose of these writings. It is to reveal the role *institution, community,* education, politics, economics, and nature have played in shaping the world of my lifetime.

One of the advantages, or disadvantages, of living seventy-plus years is that time reveals clues to the behavior of *institution* as it impacts the shaping of *community.* It is prudent for each of us to make a discerning effort to peel back the surface and explore the depths of who we are as a nation and how we came to this juncture in time. Then, we stand a better chance of making a difference in who we, as individuals, become and an even greater chance of making a difference in the world we leave behind.

America is the last stand for freedom. We must not let anyone seize the crown of hope it offers the world. To do so puts our soul at risk and allows our rational thought to diminish. We must never sacrifice our inherent goodness. When you run so fast toward your goal, you are at risk of leaving your soul behind. Then, it is time to stop and wait for your soul to catch up.

I believe running with stimulus bills, bailouts, healthcare bills, and additional stimulus bills for infrastructure projects and other such things, we are leaving behind the most critical issue the *institution* should be focusing on. Terrorism has become a great threat to America. Perhaps terrorism wouldn't be an issue if the leaders of our *institution* pondered the strategies that bear the nation's imprint of goodness and greatness. Every day there are factions abroad and within that would divide and dismantle our nation. The scary dilemma is "Political Correctness" has a stranglehold on the *institution* that was designed to support and protect the *community.* The *institution* wastes valuable time, energy, and resources on the strategy of control and turns its back on the greater issues of immigration and foreign policies. For too long, the U.S. has had a swinging-door policy that welcomed anyone onto its soil, with little discernment of their intent. It has hidden behind the constitutional term of 'freedom.' I think freedom is for all. Too often the policies of the *institution* are born out of the cry of a minute minority. Too often the *institution* operates in the extremes. When the freedoms of terrorists are of more concern than the welfare of the *community* at large, the *institution* has the obligation to implement legislation that would balance rather than abandon. To me, freedom should be extended to those who want to live in peace and harmony with the *community*. The problem with that is that politicians within the *institution* are so preoccupied with maintaining their place in the political arena, they neglect the legislative processes that would address the responsibilities of freedom. Instead, they set their cruise-control on a perpetual campaign trail. Politicians within the *institution* can be swayed by monetary rewards, favors, and gifts to treat with favor special interest groups and lobbyists. I believe the business of lobbying by special interest groups should be abolished. I am convinced that pork-barrel projects should be omitted from the budget and term limits should be put into effect. The *institution* has access to too much money - money you and I have labored to earn. With flagrant spending producing a bankrupt economy, I think it is obvious the *institution* is not a good steward of money collected from those of us in the *community*.

Unemployment is at an all time high. Once again, we've tried all kinds of ways to attack this blight on America. More people remain without jobs today than at any other time in my life. We've legislated all kinds of programs to provide for the basic needs of those who are without.

I wonder if we need to step back and explore different approaches. I ask myself how I might feel if I were out of work and with limited resources to take care of my everyday needs. Depression, sadness, and/or despondency might make a claim on my sense of worth and my ability to market myself. I'm sure my heart would be in a dark pit of hopelessness. I wonder what it might be like to create a way, several ways, to inspire and heighten individual confidence of self-worth. We budget money for all kinds of programs. The government designs all kinds of entitlement programs that may or may not have long-term energizing benefits. Why not consider what it might be like to establish classes or workshops for the purpose of reviving the spirits of those who cannot find work and whose emotional selves are spiraling downward? Maybe these could be a dramatic infusion of the wonder of being who you are. And maybe, just maybe, individuals might uncover gifts and talents that would lead to a new career path. We've got wonderful minds in America. I believe we are capable of creating opportunities that will strengthen the hearts of those who feel marginalized by our poor economy. Entitlement programs have short-term benefits that tend to take away individual self-esteem and impose lethargy and dependence. I don't know anyone who wants to surrender their sense of worth to a soup line. Most people want to lead meaningful and productive lives. Despite the poor economic circumstances in America, it remains the most lucrative nation in the world. I think it was an American novelist's philosophy that even though we live with abundance we cannot erase the sense of feeling that we no longer live nobly.

There is much that needs to be done to restore our nation to its original goodness. I have shared my views regarding the strengths of the leaders of the *institution* during my lifetime. My first proposal is to hold the leaders accountable by attitude adjustment or by the ballot box. I am convinced that it is the leaders who perpetrate division and damage the nation's sense of self. We have seen what a unified nation looks like. It was apparent in the crisis surrounding the bombing of the Murrah Building, the 9/11 attack on the World Trade Center, and other acts of terror. Now, the ball rests in the court of the *institution* and of the *community*. It is their responsibility to strive to create an equitable and unified society that respects the rights and privileges of all. Then, we will know the kind of freedom our forefather's bequeathed to us through the Constitution.

34.

As I look back over the past seventy-five years and the major happenings that influenced the evolution of the Unites States, I see some persistent threads running through the life of our nation - goodness, honor, principles, values, strength, resolve, compassion, generosity. Each of these terms and so many more define America and its wonderful people. Just like a weathered lighthouse shore beaten by the harsh swells of the ocean, these qualities have been subjected to erosion and compromise. Many of those who came here in the last fifty years came with the expectation to take from who we are with little thought, if any, to what they can give back. It never ceases to amaze me that there are those who come to soak up the 'good life' and then expect America to alter what it is to make it possible for them to live in the conventions of their homeland. They, too, are guilty of running without souls and without ingenuous expectations. If, upon crossing our shores, they discover our way of life is not congruent with their hopes, I beg them to go back home and work on securing the peace and freedom of their desires.

Asking America to compromise the values it holds dear to accommodate the wishes of its visitors is like asking a host to serve rice instead of peas. It is disrespectful and impolite and it weakens the gift of our life together. If the U.S. continues to sacrifice pieces of itself to accommodate others, there will be no 'good life.' The souls of individuals and nations are the keepers of goodness. Goodness is our moral compass. If we abdicate our soul, there will be no goodness. A world without goodness is a world that is lost in eternal despair.

35.

So how do we restore the regard for human life? A world without dignity and respect for all of life may be categorized as an imperfect world. It is one that runs without a soul or a conscience. It has been my intention to present significant evidence to this state of our national circumstance. As I have said before, the greatest crime committed by our nation is that of robbing its children of childhood. The result of which is the de-civilization of America. It spreads like cancer through all of life resulting in a very sick society. It is an infliction that lessens the quality of life as we have known it. So what is the answer to this dilemma?

The successes of our past give us reason to believe and to hope. America is a strong and powerful nation. That has been proven. More than that, it is a nation made up of great minds with blessed hearts. Were my parents alive today, most likely they would not spend much time worrying about the crisis of the world. They trusted in the grit and resilience of the people in the greatest nation ever known. You may remember reading these words earlier in my writings. It is when you discover that the lifetime of your youth can no longer be taken for granted that you begin to reflect with compassion upon the blessings of your past and search for courage to write a new script for your life.' Do not be afraid to rummage around in your past. If you don't try to re-gather from your past, it is gone forever. If you don't wonder about who and what you came from, you will never fully operate in the sunshine of your present. Sometimes delightful treasures lie hidden under dusty memories. Significance in life can be found in your remembering. The joy of living is diminished when life is so taken for granted that persons barely bother to look at its importance or to comment on it. It is when you have the courage to draw strength and wisdom from reflections of your past that you can bask in the joy of today and prepare for the challenges of tomorrow.

In a distraught world, illusions get in the way and drape a cloud of fantasy over truth. In our troubled world, we dare not live in fantasy; we might never know the joy of being alive. Life is good. The world is full of good people. There is reason to hope in a God who believes in the goodness of man and without whom the world "Runs Without a Soul."

Each of us is a guardian of the soul of America. We are blessed with good hearts that claim passions never imagined. Sift through them and commit to a journey in pursuit of the fulfillment of them. Sit with yourself in the presence of God while you wait for your soul to guide you on your journey. The preservation of America's morals and values rests with us.

Then a comparison between *institution* and *community* offers meaningful insight into their specific roles. Understanding of the values and vulnerabilities of each is helpful as we attempt to interpret the significance of the two entities. Our forefathers exercised a great deal of wisdom in their creation of the Constitution as a model of government that would inspire cooperative statesmanship, the art of compromise, and respect for human dignity and freedom. In so doing, they set in motion a system of shared participation by *institution* and *community*. I believe they knew man's propensity for power and his susceptibility to control. The Constitution is designed for a balance of power between *institution* and *community*.

For more than two hundred years, this tool has been the compass guiding the success of a democratic society. I hope these writings have given readers a look at some of the personalities and events that have eroded the fabric of the United States, disrupted the natural order in the unfolding of a society, and have continued to threaten the balance of power.

In 2008, the balance of power was disrupted when the Senate, the House of Representatives, and the President came under the control of the Democratic Party. The Republican Party was given little voice. Those of that persuasion were, in many instances, denied consideration. Just when it would seem the *institution* might be on the verge of overpowering, perhaps crushing, the *community*, a national election was held. On November 2, 2010, the Republican Party won control of the House of Representatives thereby a return to a semblance of balance. It is critical that every citizen exercise their right to vote in elections. A continuance of a balance of power is imperative if we hope to deny *institution* the opportunity to crush *community* with self-serving acts.

In these writings, I have identified *institution* and *community* as two necessary entities in human society. *Institution* - a structure to support and facilitate the needs of the society; *Community* - the society. Just as the goal of effective parenting is to protect and support the child in the process of becoming a well-adjusted, responsible individual, so the goal of the nation should be to strengthen the soul of the *community*, restore autonomy to the people, and diminish the power of the *institution*. The equation on America's marquee should read - *community* and *institution* instead of *institution* followed by *community*. This is to signify the distinction of the *community* as it dictates its needs and expectations to the *institution*. This is the paramount mission of the *community*.

The way I see it, America could benefit from an old-fashioned revival of spirit, perhaps like the ones that happened under a canvas tent in my hometown in the forties. Our nation needs a revival of it's soul. There could be singing, dancing, stories of the greatness of America, celebrating of people's accomplishments, affirmation of all ethnicities, encouragement, theater productions, etc. There could be impromptu happenings that invite *community* participation in a celebration of the commonality of who we are as a nation. They would serve as opportunities to bask in the power of the multiplicity of *community* and inspire it to greatness. Revivals awaken the senses, fill up the soul with joy and remind each of us that we are all in this thing called life together. I'd like to see us have a gigantic balloon float. The release of thousands or more bright colored balloons floating lackadaisically across the sky would give our spirits permission to soar. A more intimate revival of our spirits might happen through a personal note of gratitude. It could be a note that reminds us of the true nature of who we are.

A revival inspires people to dream outside the box of complacency. Down through the ages, it was those dreams of the extraordinary that made the United States of America the most magnificent nation in the world. America is blessed with intelligent, courageous, creative, resilient, honorable, kind people. I am proud to be in the company of those who shine a light on what is right, what is real, and what is good for all man.

It is good for a nation, blessed by God, to halt the race toward the oft-time mundane as it waits for its soul to catch up.

36.

I urge you to remember that these writings reflect my seventy-five years of life experiences. Some people will not agree with me. Many may think I am an addled old woman. Nonetheless, this is how I have perceived the evolution of life in America. I hope the visions of my past will help you navigate through the raging waters of your lives.

Much has changed in the U.S. since 1936. Once it was a warm, tender society - now fraught with terror. I think it is obvious that the leadership of the *institution* of our government has played a significant role in creating an unstable atmosphere in our nation.

The strength of America is freedom. Even though circumstances have torn at the moral and ethical fiber of America in my lifetime, there is an untapped strength in the beautiful people of our nation. America is a nation that will always search for balance, equality, and freedom. 'Freedom is not free' is a phrase with significant meaning. Great nations have great responsibilities to preserve the freedoms of all. Once America was a nation united and working in harmony for the greater good of mankind. Today, it has become a fractured conglomerate struggling to survive. A nation is like a body with many parts; no one part is greater than the other. When *institution* and *community* honor the respective gifts of each other to work in concert as a united nation, the dream of 'freedom and justice for all' will become a reality. We must become the guardians of peace as we honor the sacredness of human life which is what makes us distinct among all other nations. We must let no one seize our crown.

The United States has struggled through many losses and inflictions upon the fiber of its being. One of the first great insults to our liberty was the horrifying bombing of our ships in Pearl Harbor by The Imperial Japanese Navy on December 7, 1941. That event and others since then have been, and continue to be, callous deeds intended to daunt the resolve of our proud nation. Such phenomena were conducted at the hands of those outside our boundaries and by persons from foreign lands. Some, as in the case of the Murrah Federal Building in Oklahoma City, have been perpetuated by our own. Other such instances, have chiseled away at the values and traditions of our nation. I am remembering one act in particular that set in motion the abandonment of a sacred act honoring America. In 1963, Madelyn Murray O'Hara, a self - proclaimed atheist, brought litigation before the Supreme Court to have prayer removed from schools. The court chose to honor one atheist's demands and dismiss the beliefs of the masses. Doesn't that sound a little bit like punishing all your children for the misbehavior of one? There are some among us who would have 'In God We Trust' removed from our coins. The Pledge of Allegiance is another honoring of the nation at risk. I will never understand some of these off-the-wall, attention-getting ideas and I am glad I don't. If I did understand, it might mean I am of the same mentality as those who have nothing more to do with their time than to wound the nation that protects the rights of all it's citizens. Whether anyone likes it or not, America was founded on religious principles. I believe it is our responsibility to honor those principles.

I believe "soul" is the quiet place within the depths of man where a source of comfort, hope, and joy reside. That source I call God. Tucked within the soul is a heart; imbedded in the heart is a conscience that embraces care, that feels compassion, and that experiences pain.

There is a theory that *institution* and *community* are two necessary entities in a human society but, *institution* can be malicious because sometimes it has no heart and can crush *community*. This analogy makes sense to me.

If my hypothesis are plausible, it would make sense to me that in order for an *institution* to have a heart it must first have a soul. Soul tugs at the heart and guides the conscience. So, without a soul and without a heart and without a conscience it is almost certain that *institution* is at risk of becoming evil. *Institution's* life is contrived for the convenience of the *community*. It is to act at the pleasure of the *community*. It is governed by head-ideology. By nature; *institution* runs without a soul. On the other hand, *community* is a clustering of human life born out of a source greater than man's comprehension. I believe the soul and the heart of man rests within the source that is of God; referenced by many names; the universal God of all mankind. *Community* is driven by the yearnings of the heart. By nature *community* runs with a soul.

With this in mind, it is not difficult to imagine how leaders of *institutions* without hearts are seduced by power and fall prey to becoming evil. Think of the *institution* of government and the Presidents who serve as leaders. Compare this with the *community* whose heart is vulnerable to the callings of the conscience. *Institution* calculates with reckless abandon; *community* acts out of passion. One is of a bolder, over-powering nature; the other is of a kinder, gentler spirit. Generally, bolder actions leave a more dramatic impact upon our lives than do warm and tender ones. That is confounding, but I believe it is true.

Store tenderness and goodness in your heart like money in the bank to be shared with others, to remind you of your true nature. I am grateful, that during my life time, I have known those who have lived out of the goodness of their souls. Their lives signal the way for others to live meaningful lives - lives that make a difference in who they are and lives that inspire the goodness within the heart and soul of others. Their goodness spreads through the fiber of the world, making it a better place. My life is or has been blessed with the goodness of friends, mentors, clergy, and etc. A few months ago one of those special friends died. For more than thirty-five years,

I was blessed by both her spiritual and human existences. Her petite stature, her unassuming ambiance, and her gentle brown eyes drew others into the comfort of her presence. The passions of her soul she reserved for her family. All other passions, born out of her heart, she dedicated to making a difference in the lives of others. She heard the cries of those who were denied their right to share in the joys of living. Through the years, she shined a light of compassion upon the victims of Aids, Alzheimer's disease, poverty, and lost dreams. A special place in her heart was held for the children of Africa. Several mission trips to that country fed her hunger to ease the pain of their lives.

Days before she died, she gave each of her granddaughters a butterfly kit. They watched in hopeful anticipation as the caterpillars began to weave their cocoons then hatch as beautiful butterflies. She chose this way to help the girls grasp a vision of the transformation of her life. What a beautiful gift from her soul! Nearly five hundred people filled the sanctuary at the service memorializing her life. She lived with a clear sense of who she was and Whose she was; she never got the two confused. She defended and inspired goodness throughout the world.

Seek out friends who are good - who are moral, ethical, and decent people.

Pablo Casals said, "It takes courage for people to listen to their own goodness and act on it." That speaks to the life of my friend. I miss her presence and am grateful to have been blessed by her spirit.

I think Pablo's statement points toward the individual human condition as well as to the legalities created for the masses. That is to say, I believe that the survival of social orders is dependent upon the courage of every individual to listen to his or her goodness and to act on it. It was Julian of Norwich, 1342 - 1416, English philosopher, mystic, and theologian, who said, "Rest in the goodness of God, for that goodness reaches to the depths of our needs."

It is when there is a break from goodness that evil eases its way into being. Since social orders are framed by governments, these writings have explored the impact of the sacrifice of goodness when there is or has been little courage in society to defend it.

My friend and persons like Casals have inspired me to do what I could to be a good steward of the ethics, morals, and values embraced by society. Some will inherit the blessings of the labors. All will be sanctioned to accept the onerous challenges of preserving the integrity of what is right, what is real, and what is compassionate. It will be up to you and all others to dare to engage or deny the significance of these anchors. It is my hope some will grab the golden cord binding these gifts together and let it be the force that propels them into a bright and glorious future. You should be of good courage. You will be bearers of hope to future generations of the world.

Author's Note

In the past seven decades, I have witnessed and experienced the effects of the gradual decline of our culture. It has been as a result of conditions coloring the political, cultural, social, and educational beliefs of our nation. As a part of the Greatest Generation in the world, I am proud to have lived at a time in history characterized by stalwart unity of unwavering morals and ethics - a time marked by the success of World War II and the freeing of the oppressed in Europe and the Pacific. As I have navigated through the various generations, it has been my experience that the decline of morals and ethics in our nation is the result of political leadership, the innate struggle of each generation to lay claim to the authenticity of it's time, the fractured educational system, and man's eternal struggle to connect with an enlightened faith in a supreme being.

Today, many live with a sense of entitlement and find work to be an imposition. Sad as it may be, I believe many living in 2011 don't have a clue of what it means to live with a sense of morality. This is the state of a *community* estranged from its moral compass leaving it vulnerable to the will of the *institution*.

As the *institution* of government has escalated its desires for power, the *community* has courageously battled for freedom and peace. When the *institution* claims power and authority over the *community*, fear ignites in the heart of *community* forcing it to fight for survival. This is the interminable struggle that exists between the *institution* and the *community* of the United States of America. In the smoldering ashes of our burning society, is a cultural decline of morals and ethics that undermines the common decency of man's respect for humanity. In the soil of the soul, is the educational dilemma that denies the significance of childhood and the role it plays in the nurturing of mentally healthy, responsible human beings who are guardians of the societies belonging to our times. I take heart in that it appears there is evidence of a revival of Christianity on the horizon of America. It is my hope this is indicative of the nation having come full circle and the evolution of a more principled society emerging in the future.

Last week when I visited the Oklahoma State Fair, I stopped at the huge butterfly tent. Hundreds of butterflies of all colors flitted about, from a butterfly bush to a fresh cut melon to a bowl of sweet honey water, drinking up life sustaining nectar. Inside parents were teaching their children what happens when you stand perfectly still among these beautiful creatures. Some had the privilege of having a butterfly light on their shoulder. Others had one land on an extended forefinger. Another had a butterfly rest on the tip of his nose. There were those who found it difficult to wait with quiet restraint for the wispy touch of a butterfly. Parents were teaching their children the difference between what can happen when you stand still or when you race about. Sometimes standing still is the best thing you can do. When you are still you can enjoy the beauty of what is around you. When you dart about you deny the blessings of all that surrounds you. These loving parents were helping their children savor the reverence, and delight imprinted upon their hearts. Preserving childhood is a commitment society must make if it hopes to restore the morals and ethics of our culture. To do less puts the nation at risk of Running Without A Soul.

The Good News is that America is a God-loving nation. It is a *community* that seeks excellence. The nurturing of our young, the preserving of childhood, and the demand for education that grows a moral society challenges each and everyone of us. America is a democratic society that operates under a well-defined Constitution that invites the citizenry to claim an active role in the preservation of freedom. The intention is that *institution* and *community* shall serve as the axis of power that guides society toward 'liberty and justice' for all. When that happens, we will know what it means to live in a country that courageously breathes new life into the meaning of the words: 'A government of the people, by the people, and for the people.'

Friends and family, my mantra to you: Let no one seize your crown. Let no one take away the beauty and goodness of who you are. Your presence in this world is not an accident. You have as much right to be here in this time and in this place as anyone on this planet. Make no doubt about it, you are special, but no more special than anyone else. Your thoughts and ideas are as valid as the next person's. Don't be afraid to appropriately share them with others. Play fair. Honor the sacredness of life. Love deeply and fill each day with happiness and joy. Know that you are a child of a Holy God who blesses you with His promise to be with you always. In the biblical book of John we are reminded that Christ is the Vine and we are the branches. That means we are to be Christ Followers, not Leaders of the pack. When we surrender our life-giving, life-sustaining spiritual life with the Vine for the expediency of human life we experience a divine disconnect like a branch fallen to the ground or young adults untethered in the *Summer of Love*, or a young girl left behind in the watermelon patch. In today's world, I wonder if our youth are more tethered to cell phones, I Pads, and computers than to the God within. When our race is interrupted by tragedy, crisis, or illness, there is a danger of racing through life alone. In that gnawing moment, we look back over our shoulders in despair to summon "Are you running with me Jesus? Please tell me you are still with me. Where are you, God?"

Last week, our minister, shared this story:

It seems Bill Green, a Pastor of a Church in Chicago, tells that after he finished presenting a conference in Germany, Rolf, his translator, who has been a very good friend for twenty years, drove the Pastor to the airport in Frankfort. Rolf loves fast cars and on the autobahn he was wanting to give Bill a thrill in his very fast car. That morning opened to a light misty rain and not a lot of traffic. For a while, as they drove to the airport, they were having a real, connecting spiritual conversation. Parts of the autobahn are speed restricted, where the kilometers per hour would be 70 or 80 K - only 49 to 56 miles per hour through towns. While in the lower, restricted speed zones, they were talking in spiritual ways about God in their lives. While talking that way, they arrived at the unrestricted part of the autobahn and Rolf put the hammer down. It was a very fast car and only registers kilometers per hour. Bill noticed that when they got to 140, 150, 160, they had less conversation with each other. And when we passed 200 kilometers per hour we were totally quiet. And at about 240 kilometers per hour, Bill said, "I started an internal conversation in my head, mainly thoughts about my eternity." He pegged that car at 250 kilometers, that's 175 miles per hour, in the rain - and it was extremely quiet in the car! Then the speed limit zones came back into view and they slowed way down. Green said that it was very interesting to him as soon as the speed limit zones slowed their speed, they began talking again. What a perfect metaphor. When your life gathers speed, higher, higher, higher, there is some point at which conversation stops between ourselves and God because our mind is on other stuff. Going too fast to read your Bible, too fast to keep your heart tuned to God to ask the risen Christ for guidance, too fast to have a low, soulful conversation with our spouse, and the kids are just a nuisance then we are going too fast. We can have velocity but it can yield barrenness of spiritual life.

This story is a glaring analogy of the compromised condition of the soul of America. As we garner speed, we are numbed to the sacredness of life. When we violate the great laws of nature, life as we have known it, is jaded. A nation that sacrifices reverence, respect, common decency for expediency of the race is at risk of losing the life blood that sustains it.

Years ago I read a story whose theme pointed to man's existence in the world. The author drew on his spiritual linkage when he proclaimed, as persons of faith, 'We are called to live in the world; not to become creatures of the world.' I can't help wondering if in our reckless abandon toward the future we stand between the juncture of these two. Who and whose will we choose to become? This is a question we ponder. We must sit upon a rock while we wait for our souls to catch up.

We wait with anticipation for life emerging from the cocoon. Is it:

A hungry caterpillar?

A beautiful butterfly?

Or something in between?

Acknowledgements

Dreams are born out of the soul and ushered into reality with the help of those who wish us well. I was blessed by family and friends who embraced this dream.

My dear friend, Billie Terlip, believed in me and had confidence in my work. She offered encouragement when I was faint in heart.

My sister, Dr. Eleanor Joan Kopper and my friend, Bob Gentry graciously took time away from their busy schedules to read my work.

Special thanks go to my daughter, Michelle Brecht, who patiently listened to my musings. My granddaughter, Mickenzie Bush, who created the graphic design on the cover of the book while her husband, Gary Bush led my cheering section. Go, Grammy!

To my husband, Larry L. Miles, who edited this manuscript more times than I can count, I say thanks. He held the keys to the authenticity of my writings and called me to clarity. This would have been less meaningful were it not for his faith in my dream, his trust in my work, his enduring patience, his abiding devotion, and his strident assessments. I am humbled by his warm presence.

Every dream needs a generous sprinkling of 'gold dust' to shine upon the passions of the soul. A big thanks to my 'Dream Makers.'

CPSIA information can be obtained at www.ICGtesting.com
Printed in the USA
LVOW090708290612

287977LV00001B/4/P